Dear Reader,

How often is it said that we never ask e͟r͟ *parents while they are still around to answer them?*

Olive Rees

Ivor Rees

Ern Hayward

Jack Newbury

The Swansea Imperial Singers began life in 1938 as an octet of working comrades who sang together in their lunch-hour.

After World War II the choir expanded into an accomplished seventeen strong, male-voice ensemble which flourished, under the expert leadership and tutorship of their conductor, Jack Newbury, into one of South Wales' most popular choirs.

They performed together locally, and broadcast nationally across the radio airwaves through the tumultuous years of the 1930s, 1940s and 1950s.

Many of the things we should like to know about them remain out of reach, owing to the passage of time, but our little book tries to convey the story of this vibrant choir and the town that they loved, through the lives of some of its members – our parents, uncles, and grandparents who performed for the love of song.

'I do not ask for a luxurious life

the world's gold or its fine pearls

I ask for a happy heart,

an honest heart, a pure heart.'

(from 'Calon Lan')

Contents

Stave 1 - What's in a name?   2

Stave 2 - 'Britain's greatest male ensemble'   4

Stave 3 - North American adventures   12

Stave 4 - 'Colliers, engineers and clerks'   20

Stave 5 - The Swansea Imperials   25

Stave 6 - Imperials at War   36

Stave 7 - The Three Nights' Blitz   44

Stave 8 - American invasion   54

Stave 9 - 'Radio fun'   62

Stave 10 - A special year   72

Stave 11 - Waxing lyrical   85

Stave 12 - Swan song   93

Acknowledgements   101

Appendix - More Imperials!   105

'Unlocking the past' by Geoff Rees   112

Stave 1

'What's in a name?'

Ern Hayward

Tal Griffiths

Jack Newbury

Olive Rees

Ivor Rees

Where did that name come from? We had never thought to ask them.

'All my life I had just believed that the Singers, many of whom worked at Swansea's ICI Landore plant, had simply taken the name 'Imperial' from 'Imperial Chemical Industries'. But then, at the beginning of 2019, when I first made contact with my co-authors, I was to make an astonishing discovery ...

... For the Swansea Imperials were not the first to adopt this grand title – there had been an earlier choir of that name with a truly extraordinary story ... (Geoff Rees).

...'The Welsh Imperial Singers'...

... and for reasons, which shall quickly become obvious, our narrative must begin with them ...

Stave 2

'Britain's greatest male ensemble'...

Let us take you back in time ... nearly 100 years ...

for in the mid 1920s, celebrated tenor, conductor and musician,
R. Festyn Davies, from Trawsfynydd in North Wales,
had the idea of recruiting a male ensemble comprising singers
from all over his homeland and from all walks of life.

If his short-term aim was to take this choir on a tour of Great Britain, his long-term plan was for the choir to undertake an ambitious and extensive programme of concerts in North America, where he had already spent a considerable part of his successful musical career.

He intended that everything about the choir would be exceptional – even the way they presented themselves on stage.

The new choir, 'The Welsh Imperial Singers', would be **attractively dressed in old Welsh red Regency-style swallow-tailed coats, decorative waistcoats and fob chains, frilled white jabots and buff trousers**.

To complement the appearance of the choir while remaining distinctive, Festyn Davies would wear a similar jacket, but brown in colour, and knee breeches. He decided membership of the choir would be by invitation or recommendation only, and every singer would be admitted only with a full C.V of achievement. This new and exciting choir's first concert was scheduled for October 1926.

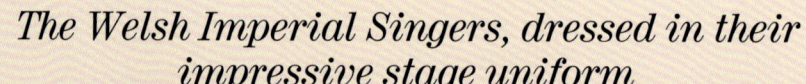

The Welsh Imperial Singers, dressed in their impressive stage uniform

Festyn Davies Jack Newbury

(Photo courtesy of Gwasg Carreg Gwalch)

1926

In that year, all the talk in Swansea had been of sport and singing. In March, **Swansea Town had reached the F.A. Cup semi-finals, having disposed of the 'mighty Arsenal' in the quarter-finals at the Vetch Field.** In the same month, Wales were defeating an otherwise all-conquering Irish XV at St. Helen's in front of 40,000 fans, more than 5,000 of whom had travelled from the Emerald Isle.

In April, on Pendine Sands, J.B. Parry Thomas was breaking the World Land Speed Record in his car 'Babs'

© Trinity Mirror/Mirrorpix/Alamy Stock Photo

Later in the year, in the first week of August, the **Australlan Touring Cricket Team were facing Glamorgan, also at the iconic St. Helen's ground, in front of 20,000 spectators, while, just a few hundred yards away, thousands more were attending the Welsh National Eisteddfod.**

However, not everything was so joyful in South Wales. In May of that year the **National General Strike was called, and there was constant strife in the coalfields across the Principality.** The economy was gradually sinking towards the grim years of the Depression with low wages and high levels of unemployment. Although Swansea was not as badly hit as the Valleys and East Wales, local newspapers feature pictures of soup kitchens set up for out-of-work miners, and in the following years, unemployed men and sometimes whole families on charity-funded trips to Gower and Porthcawl.

Jack Newbury in 1926 as a newly recruited member of the Welsh imperial Singers in full stage dress.

Jack Newbury

It may have been against this backdrop that one ambitious, twenty-two year-old singer from Swansea decided to seize the opportunity of a life time when invited to join Festyn Davies' ensemble.

Jack Newbury became the only West Walian member of the choir which originally featured 21 singers. It is noticeable that Tom Lloyd, another member of the new choir, had won the bass baritone prize at the Swansea Eisteddfod. Might Jack and Tom have conversed at this time ? The attraction to a young man setting out in life of being paid to do what he most loved must have been almost irresistible, let alone the promise of touring, not just the United Kingdom, but the world!

Jack's was a musical family. His older brother had played the bugle in the Boys' Brigade; his younger sister Eva Mary Newbury was, in later years, to tour Australia with the prestigious D'Oyly Carte Opera Company, while his younger brother Frank would become a member of the Swansea Imperials and other choirs. While they were children and teenagers, the siblings' evening entertainment frequently included singing together around the family piano.

We cannot be sure of how Jack came to learn of the Welsh Imperials, but Frank Newbury, then thirteen years old, recalled in later life how R. Festyn Davies had come to their family home in Iorwerth Street, Manselton, Swansea to give Jack 'and others' a singing test in the front parlour. Jack was selected and the project proceeded at top speed. **The first rehearsals of the 'Welsh Imperial Singers' were held in September, 1926, less than a month after the Eisteddfod!**

So began an extraordinary flurry of activity with the choir's first concert to be presented in Anglesey just one month later.

Amazingly, another 21 performances were made in the month following, and the choir rapidly built a repertoire of over 100 items, ranging from Welsh airs to Operatic arias that they could perform with ease on any occasion.

Jack was already a very accomplished 'basso profundo', as can be ascertained from early concert programmes for the choir which itemise each singer's individual performance pieces. **Jack's highlights included 'O Isis and Osiris' and 'In Hallow'd Dwellings' from Mozart's 'The Magic Flute'; 'Asleep in the Deep' by Petrie; 'See the Heavens Smile' by Purcell; 'The Lute Player' by Allitsen; 'When a Maiden' from 'Il Seraglio' by Mozart, and 'The Road to Anywhere' by Ashleigh.** These programmes also feature the duets, 'When I Survey', and 'Vale' (Farewell) sung by Jack in harmony with R.T. Williams, a celebrated baritone from near Llangollen.

If this was not enough evidence of Jack's prowess, he was also singled out for individual praise in newspaper reviews, such as the following extract from **'The Western Mail' in October 1926**:

The Choir 'possesses some remarkable soloists, notable amongst whom must be mentioned Jack Newbury, one of the finest basses I have heard in recent years, rich in vocal timbre, controlled, and of lovely suaveness of vocal line which detracts nothing from vocal vigour

After a concert in Colwyn Bay in December 1926, **'The North Wales Weekly News'** music correspondent wrote that,

People marvelled at the fine and pure deep bass of Mr Jack Newbury, who thrilled them by his version of 'O Isis and Osiris' (from Mozart's 'Magic Flute') ... The duet 'When I survey' was so magnificently sung by Messrs Jack Newbury and R.T. Williams that the audience found it difficult to curb its enthusiasm.

The same correspondent greatly admired Festyn Davies' style of conducting – flamboyant but not overly so, deflecting the attention from himself to his singers. The arrangement of the choir on stage was 'picturesque but also musically effective' and the concert seemed to move forward from item to item seamlessly.

Billed as **'21 of Wales' Finest Artistes'**, the Imperials visited dozens of towns and cities

The **choir embarked on a nationwide tour of over 250 concerts in the next twelve months**. Billed as '21 of Wales' Finest Artistes', the Imperials visited dozens of towns and cities, including London, Birmingham, Manchester, Stratford-Upon-Avon, Southampton and Liverpool, and sang in front of such worthies as The Duke of York (the future King George V1) and David Lloyd George. Every concert concluded with stirring renditions of 'Land of My Fathers' followed by 'God Save the King'.

In August 1927, Frank Newbury, who was very fond and proud of his older brother, proved his own supreme athleticism by cycling the 45 miles from Swansea to Brecon across the formidable, western heights of the Beacons on his three-speed Sturmy Archer bike. His aim was to be able to see and hear Jack and the Singers during their week of concerts in the town. Frank's wonderfully exhausting act of devotion was repaid in full by the brilliance of what he heard. His verdict on the choir's performance was one of complete admiration for their quality and professionalism. 'In these days of anything goes,' he recalled, 'it is nice to remember the discipline of the Singers... **The press came to describe my brother as the Chaliapin of Wales'.**

1927

'**The Brecon Times**' fully endorsed Frank's assessment,

The celebrated Welsh Imperial Singers, who have been providing Brecon people with the opportunity of hearing some really excellent singing at the Town Hall during the past three nights, are remaining in the town until the end of the week. All who have heard this company have nothing but praise for their remarkably fine musical expression, their wonderful discipline and their undoubted enthusiasm.

'O Isis and Osiris'

This famous aria has always been a 'test piece' for singers of especially low voices. It comes from Mozart's last opera, 'The Magic Flute' (1791), which premiered in Vienna just two months before the composer's premature death.

It is sung by the character, Sarastro, a benevolent priest, who invokes the Egyptian gods, Isis and Osiris, asking them to protect the hero and heroine of the opera, Tamino and Pryina.

The extraordinary vocal range of the original singers for whom Mozart tailored his music poses great difficulties for those who have since attempted the roles.

However, Jack was the complete master of this particular musical challenge.

Stave3

North American
adventures

1928

In September 1928, fourteen of the choir set out by cruise liner from Liverpool to Quebec to begin their first overseas tour.

The itinerary covered the entire breadth of Canada and lasted a remarkable 10 months ! They were welcomed by Welsh societies everywhere, and received invitations to sing in churches, large halls, big department stores, Sunday schools, colleges and on Canadian radio.
Each singer was paid a basic salary of £3 – 15s shillings per week, plus expenses, but it seems they could earn considerably more in small bonuses.

The **choir returned to Great Britain at the end of May 1929,** but the Canadian venture had been such a great success that, less than four months later, the Welsh Imperials set forth again across the Atlantic – **this time to attempt a twenty month tour of Canada and the United States by train and bus.**

The Welsh Imperials performed in Montreal, Toronto, Calgary, towns of The Rockies, and in British Columbia.

1929

Now billed as **'Britain's Greatest Male Ensemble'**, the choir sang before vast audiences in Chicago, New York State, Pennsylvania, Missouri, Illinois, and Iowa, as well as in the multiple small venues along the way.

One tenor who performed with the choir throughout its existence and made all five New World tours was Watkin Edwards, a veteran of World War I.
Watkin wrote a regular and colourful commentary on the tours which was published in his home town newspaper in North Wales. Such was the popularity of the choir that Watkin believed the Welsh Imperials were bringing Wales to the notice of the World.

In some of the casual photographs of the second tour, Jack is featured jauntily wearing a pair of plus fours, and, on one occasion, some football kit in readiness for a friendly match with a college team, proving that these New World adventures were not all work and no play.

> **The choir began its third tour** of the North American Continent in June 1931.

Once again the tour brought great acclaim from all who saw the brilliant Welshmen and, after barely five weeks back at home, the choir began its third tour of the North American Continent in June 1931. This comprised concerts not only in familiar venues, but also in those states in the U.S not previously visited, such as Ohio, North and South Dakota, Vermont, Oklahoma, Kentucky, Tennessee, Alabama, Georgia and Florida. They added Vaudeville Theatres to their itinerary, on one occasion meeting the famous Hollywood star Will Rogers.

The Imperials often stayed at the homes of Welsh ex-pats. Phil Newbury, Jack's son, recalls his father being inundated with cards and presents, parcels of chocolate, chewing-gum and adventure comics from good friends made in America, long after his visits there.

Returning home in April 1932, the choir once again took only a brief break of a few weeks before heading back to The States on their fourth tour in July. On Jack's recommendation, another Swansea singer joined the group. He was Ivor Evans who eventually became principal bass at Sadler's Wells Opera.

1932

Although a collection of excellent individuals, the Imperials happily shared their place in the sun, advising and encouraging one another and exchanging musical pieces. Within Jack's portfolio of sheet music is a gentle melody, **'When the House is Asleep', given to him by fellow bass Ulam Hughes from North Wales.**

Over the next six months The Welsh Imperials performed in thirteen States, covering huge distances on sometimes poor roads across the Continent, in a bus, which, on occasions, proved stubborn and unreliable. **But America was now in the throes of the Depression with millions out of work**. Invitations for the Welsh Imperials to perform and cover their expenses were fewer and the tour was ended prematurely in January 1933. Back in Wales, there a was a forlorn attempt to make a film for Paramount which included the Imperials as singing quarrymen, but dreadful weather called a halt to the enterprise.

© Everett Collection/Shutterstock

World War I veterans boarding a bus taking them from New York City's Battery to Fort Slocum, about 40 miles away for dollar-a-day jobs at government's reforestation camp.

Although another tour of the USA was attempted in 1938 – 9 under Festyn Davies' direction, only four of the original Welsh Imperials participated. **Jack Newbury left the choir in 1934. He had a tempting offer to join an opera company in London, but decided to return to his home town.**

Was this a decision to find a more stable job and settle down in a time of great economic uncertainty? **Was it homesickness, or simply a reaction to the hugely tiring fourth tour?**

Perhaps the answer can be found in a recently rediscovered postcard sent by maestro, Festyn Davies, to Jack, which is featured on the facing page. It illustrates the great respect that the conductor had for his 'basso profundo', but it also helps to explain why Jack had opted out of another punishing tour of North America. **The card is dated Christmas Day, 1938,** when the Welsh Imperials were in the midst of their fifth and final visit to the States. They were staying at **The Stevens – 'the World's largest Hotel' – in Chicago, a 3000 room giant built in the late 1920s,** with an amazing view over Grant Park and Lake Michigan and with the integrated facilities of a small city. The choir gave many concerts in 'The Windy City' during the 1930s.

Once again the choir had travelled vast distances across the Continent. Despite their 'tremendous' popularity, RFD, (signing himself 'Uncle', the affectionate nickname by which the choir knew him), seems to be intimating that the Singers were only making enough money to cover their costs. Even so, he was optimistic that he had prepared the way for yet another more successful and lucrative tour in the second half of 1939.

Perhaps Festyn Davies had intended the card to tempt Jack to undertake one last trip, reminding him of his great popularity amongst the communities they had visited on previous visits –'Hundreds had asked me about you'. RFD knew that the Americans loved not only Jack's wonderful voice but his down to earth charm, warmth, and exuberant personality.

Far from being 'crippled', we learn that Jack had married his adored fiancée, Carrie (April 1938) and that they had set up home in Bath Road, Morriston soon after.

There was nothing RFD could say to lure him back. As we know from hindsight, the prospects of a 1939 tour were doomed from the start and it never took place.

The 1938 visit was not the only time the choir had stayed at this prestigious venue. 'The Stevens Hotel' was truly a 'city within a city', with accommodation for 3,600 guests, employing 2,500 staff, with a ballroom 'adorned like the Palace of Versailles', a library, a hospital, bowling alley, barber shop, rooftop miniature golf course, theatre, ice-cream shop and drug-store.

The Singers sang in the famous 'Gold Room' of the hotel during their visits there. Every President of the USA since 1930 and many other important visitors such as Tony Blair and Frank Sinatra have been guests at The Stevens, now renamed as 'The Conrad Hilton'.

Front of the card

'We have had a break this Christmas. Singing twice at this Hotel & naturally had room accommodation over Xmas. RFD'.

'Dear Jack,

Just a line to wish you a 'Happy New Year'. I miss you on this tour.
We have travelled over 16,000 miles by bus since 1st of Oct.

Just keep my head so far and that's all, although we have made a tremendous hit everywhere. Hundreds asked me about you. I said you were crippled – married – but happy.

I think I have laid a fine foundation for next year – it was like starting afresh this trip.

All the best, love to all, from your red friend (a reference to the choir's red jackets)'.

Uncle R. Festyn Davies

Modern readers, used to world-wide travel, may not wonder at the Welsh Imperials' adventures across the Atlantic, but these **momentous journeys were undertaken in the 1920s and 1930s, when it took seven days to cross the ocean and involved mind-boggling travelling distances in the New World**. The tours, packed with concerts, were hard, and gruelling at times but left the participants with a range of experiences and memories of which the average working man in Wales, even in 2022, can only dream.

Back in Swansea, **Jack was to form his very own group of talented singers, who eventually would come to be known as 'The Swansea Imperial Singers'** and they were to benefit greatly from the extraordinary range of musical knowledge and experience that Jack had absorbed during his association with R. Festyn Davies and his remarkable All-Wales ensemble.

(*To discover more about the Welsh Imperials see Alun Trevor's brilliant history of this exceptional choir, published by Gwasg Carreg Gwalch. He describes it as a 'scrapbook' but it is absolutely a treasure trove of precious memories and photographs, and pen pictures of all the participants which should be better known by everyone in Wales. Alun's father, Jabez Trevor, was an outstanding tenor who was a stalwart of the choir*).

Jack may have been drawn back to Swansea for romantic reasons, but his home town had become a musical powerhouse in his absence.

In 1934 The Swansea and District Royal Male Voice Choir won first prize in the Eisteddfod competition for large choirs held at Neath. The fun, the joy and the exhilaration that choral singing brought to so many men of South Wales during those grim years of the 1930s cannot be better illustrated than by the extraordinary Evening Post photograph of the triumphant choir on the facing page.

Conductor Ivor Owen had been unable to stay at Neath to hear the result as he had been contracted to lead an Urdd party of over 600 people aboard the cruise liner 'Orduna' on a tour which was to visit Brittany, Spain, Portugal and West Africa. The Urdd travellers included 102 people called 'Jones'!

Mayhem at High Street Station!

On his return to Swansea High Street he was
ambushed and serenaded by as many of his choir who
could squeeze themselves onto the platform.
In the photograph the conductor displays a playful side
of his character as he stands centre picture, bronzed
and wearing a Basque Country beret at a jaunty angle,
completely besieged by his delighted singers.
Pinned on Ivor Owen's breast is the white ribbon that was
the much-sought-after emblem of victory...

... and there, kneeling at his side, is a talented young
tenor, who , as we shall see, was to become a life-long
working and musical friend of the returning
Jack Newbury, Geoff Rees' father, Ivor Rees.

Stave 4

'Colliers, engineers and clerks'

Swansea Male-Voice at
The Metropole Hotel in Llandrindod Wells

1937

The first reference that we have found to a 'Swansea Imperial' choir is from 1938, but what was Jack doing musically between this time and leaving The Welsh Imperials in 1934?

Two photographs have come to light in Geoff's parents' collection which may offer the solution, each dating from July 1937.

"They had stopped at the famous hostelry for refreshments and had treated hotel guests to a few songs from their repertoire. The prestigious choir's itinerary also included stops at Brecon, Devil's Bridge and Aberystwyth. Jack Newbury stands very prominently in the second row with a large flower in his lapel, but the photograph includes many other men who were to become members of the Swansea Imperials, including my father, Ivor Rees, and John Hayward's father, Ernest.

The first photograph at the top of this page features the entire Swansea and District Royal Male-Voice Choir on their annual outing and was taken at the Metropole Hotel in Llandrindod Wells.

1937

The second photograph, probably taken on the same outing in July, 1947, is of a smartly-suited section of The Swansea and District Royal Male-voice Choir.
Jack Newbury (1)
Hugh Cann MBE (2)
Frank Newbury (3)
George Owen (4)
Ivor Rees (5)

In this group are Hugh Cann who was to become the Swansea Imperials' President after World War II, and Jack's handsome younger brother Frank who was also blessed with a fine voice. While Jack had been touring the New World, Frank had been busy studying at Dynevor Grammar School, situated in the centre of Swansea. He progressed well there, but, as for many of his generation, the harsh economic realities meant that he had to leave school at the age of fourteen to find work.

Frank joined the Post Office delivering telegrams, which were an important means of communication for businesses before many of them had telephones. Frank would recount the salutary tale of how he was taken down to the Central Post Office in Swansea on his first day of work by his mother, where he saw a young man leaving in tears. That man had failed his entrance exam and had to leave his employment.

Frank, however. Had no difficulty in qualifying when his time came. Save for his years in War Service, he was to remain with the Post Office throughout his working life, retiring as a senior manager.

© Pictorial Press Ltd/Alamy Stock Photo

Having recovered from their exhausting excursion, three days later, on the 14th July 1937, the choir, under conductor Ivor Owen, sang before the new **King, George VI** and **Queen Elizabeth** in Swansea's Brangwyn Hall. A vivid contemporary account of the royal visit appears on page 24.

One could claim that the 1930s were 'a golden age' for singing in Swansea. Contemporary photographs of the celebrated, large, male-voice choirs prove their huge popularity despite, perhaps even because of these colourless times of economic hardship. Swansea, Morriston United and the newly-formed Morriston Orpheus, dominated the prestigious prize for over 80 voices at the Welsh National Eisteddfods during the pre-World War II decade.

Jack Newbury, Ernest Hayward, always known as 'Ern', Frank Newbury and Geoff's father, Ivor Rees were immensely proud of their participation in the 'Swansea Male Voice' and they made many friends there, some of whom would become stalwart members of the Swansea Imperials.

However, having worked with a group of such brilliant individuals in the Welsh Imperials, Jack's ambition was to create his own small choir in order to have greater flexibility to perform a wider programme of music, and where greater emphasis could be placed on discipline and technique.

'THE EVENING POST' REPORTED,'...

(Article quoted courtesy of South Wales Evening Post)

the black-coated Swansea and District Male Voice Choir, with the conductor, Mr Ivor Owen, at the organ, filled the stage at the far end. 'Hen Wlad fy Nhadau' was sung to fine effect, and the presentations by the Mayor to their Majesties proceeded quickly, so that there would be some time for the inspection of the Brangwyn panels ...

... Then came a departure from programme. The town clerk fetched Mr Ivor Owen, who came from the stage and was presented. The King asked the age and constitution of the choir, and was told that it was formed

37 years ago, was composed of 'colliers, engineers and clerks', and had sung before Royalty thrice previously.

Their Majesties thought the singing, and especially the tone, very beautiful, and his Majesty asked for 'Ash Grove'. This folk song, unrehearsed, was sung in Welsh, its tiniest whisperings reaching to fine effect through the hall.

Their Majesties sat with the Mayor and Mayoress centrally, about a third of the way down the hall, and at the end the Queen walked up to the platform and thanked Mr Owen with a charming 'Diolch yn Fawr'.

The Queen added: 'It was very sweet. We wish we could remain here an hour. I think the choir sings most beautifully.'

Then there was the most moving period of all – the singing of the National Anthem, with an extra verse for the Queen.

It sounded like a prayer, the motionless gathering was gripped: and then, at a call from the ranks of the councillors, there were three cheers as the King and Queen and their retinue passed out to their journey to the station.'

Stave 5

The Swansea Imperials!

Photo courtesy of Swansea Council: Swansea Museum Collection

At the beginning of World War II, more than 2,500 men and women were employed in Landore.

As we have intimated in an earlier chapter, we believed for many years that the choir had **derived its name from the 'Imperial' of Imperial Chemical Industries**, whose huge plant occupied almost the entire area of the Lower Swansea Valley. Many of the men who were to sing in the choir were employed by ICI, including Jack Newbury himself who had returned to work there as a machine-tool fitter.

At the beginning of World War II, more than 2,500 men and women were employed in Landore. The area had been the focus of the most important copper industry in the World during the 19th century, and by the 1890s, the lower Swansea Valley housed the greatest concentration of metallurgical industries in Europe. By the mid 1930s, the two largest concerns, the Hafod and the Morfa Works had merged with several other smaller factories to create one large, integrated complex and the factories now focused on the production of copper, brass and alloy sheets for markets as far ranging as India.

In 2022, little evidence remains of the ICI works. Swansea City and Ospreys fans parking in the Landore Park and Ride, and strolling in and around the 'Swansea.com Stadium', probably never give a thought as to what had previously occupied the land. When the factories closed, the copper and metallurgical industries left behind a legacy of dereliction and industrial waste, and in the 1960s the Council began an almost total clearance project to rid the landscape of the chimneys, rolling mills, factory buildings and the enormous copper slag tip with its black dunes that once stood along Pentremawr Road and where the, present-day, Pentrehafod Comprehensive School stands.

The common, modern impression of life in the Valley as it existed in the 1930s is one of hardship and pollution, but these **works gave employment and comradeship to tens of thousands of workers over the years, and many men from that era have recorded their nostalgic memories of their time there**. During this period of the Depression in Wales, to have a job at the works was a privilege indeed.

One such ICI man was Andrea Davies' **grandfather, Taliesin Griffiths, or 'Tal'** as he liked to be known. Nine years older than Jack, Tal was the youngest of nine children born in Crown Street, Morriston in 1895, in a house that his father had built, and where he lived for most of his life. He worked as a pattern maker in the ICI – 'the best employer that I knew'. Living close by, Tal was a frequent visitor to Jack's home in Bath Road, Morriston and an influence on the choir's choice of musical repertoire and arrangements.

Similarly, another of Jack's work colleagues, Geoff's father **Ivor Rees, was to become an important member of the choir**. Born in March 1910, and brought up in a terraced house in Sydney Street in Brynhyfryd, the descendant of several generations of miners, Ivor had managed to escape the treacherous conditions of the local collieries in which his father and uncles had worked and suffered, and, upon leaving school, he had found an opening as an office-boy at ICI under one of its former titles.

His fine tenor voice was noted at an early age as he sang in chapels and churches in the area, and **by the age of 20, he was a member of the renowned Swansea and District Choir.**

During this period of the Depression in Wales, to have a job at the works was a privilege

Tal Griffiths

Following the profile of most of the Imperials, **Tal was already a fine singer, and belonged to several other local choirs in his lifetime** – Morriston Orpheus, the B.B.C. Singers – as well as being one of the **founder members of The Swansea Imperials.**

Ivor Rees

In 1925, Ivor began an apprenticeship as a machine tool fitter – he was to work for **ICI for 47 years – but in his private life his great love was of singing.**

1930s

During the 1930s the excursions organised by Works or Chapels were a very popular form of break for working-class families.

The B.C.M (ICI) Engineering Department on a works outing. This photo was taken in Barry, on the Saturday before Whit Monday in 1933. Ivor Rees is pictured standing, holding his trilby, third from the left.

1936

The members of Manselton Congregational Church pictured before they embarked on their August Bank Holiday outing to Elan Valley and Aberystwyth.

©aboikis/Shutterstock

My parents' wedding day 1936

My parents, **Ivor Rees and Olive Annie Jenkins**, on their wedding day, 8th February, 1936.

Like many other choristers of whom we shall read, my father was a very talented and intelligent man, forced only by economic circumstances and accident of birth to leave education early. Amongst my collection of books, I still possess many of the classics which Dad bought second-hand as a young man – works ranging from Jane Austen's 'Northanger Abbey' to a complete set of brown, leather-bound Dickens' novels. I can't imagine that he read them all, but they signify his great belief in and respect for culture and self-improvement.

Ivor met my mother, Olive Annie Jenkins, at Manselton Congregational Chapel. Mum was living with her parents only a light step away in Hoskins Terrace, Pentregethin Road, and she and my Dad were married at the Chapel in February 1936. This was a particularly happy union for the future Swansea Imperials, because **my mother was a skilful and versatile pianist**, who could turn her hand to classical, choral, operatic, and light-operatic pieces. She became the choir's very popular resident accompanist for its duration, and I can fully understand why. My mother was simply the calmest, sweetest and most patient person I have ever known. In her heart of hearts she was a romantic and an enthusiastic fan of the movies, whether musicals or adventures. Her favourite matinee idol was the cool, handsome and sophisticated English actor Robert Donat, and her favourite film 'The Thirty-Nine Steps'. **Geoff Rees**

My father was a very talented and intelligent man, forced only by economic circumstances and accident of birth to leave education early

my mother was a skilful and versatile pianist, who could turn her hand to classical, choral, operatic, and light-operatic pieces

The **Swansea Imperial Octet** in 1938.
Back row (left to right):
Ivor Rees, Ben Davies,
George Owen,
Jack Newbury,
Tal Griffiths.
Front row (left to right):
Emlyn Morgan,
Olive Rees, Cecil Lewis.

In the great, time-honoured tradition of miners and factory employees **many of the ICI men not only worked, but sang together on the job.**

In November 1938, eight of them, including Jack, Taliesin and Ivor, who had been practising together in their lunch-breaks, decided to go further, and in heart-warming, storybook fashion, form their very own small, performance choir, naming themselves **'The Swansea Imperial Octet'**. From this wonderfully whimsical beginning, one of South Wales' most popular male-voice choirs of the 1940s and early 1950s was to emerge.

Less than twelve months after their formation, on 16th August, 1939, 'The Evening Post' was reporting,

'The Swansea Imperial Octet ... which has given several concerts for local charities, will broadcast for the first time from Swansea at 9.30 this evening.

The Octet is made up of the following male singers: Messrs Gwyn Thomas, Emlyn Morgan, Ivor Rees, Ben Davies, Cecil Lewis, George Owen, Jack Newbury and Tal Griffiths. Accompanist is Madam Ivor Rees (LRAM)'.

They were nearly all colleagues at ICI, and drawn from all quarters of the factory-floor and office staff. Cecil Lewis, for instance, was a foreman with a life-long love of singing.

9.30 10.00 Wythawd Imperial Abertawe –
The Swansea Imperial Octet.
Conductor Gwyn Thomas

Down in Yon Summer Vale	Charles Wood
In Silent Night, Lullaby	Brahms
An Evening's Pastorale	Wilfred Shaw
Little Tommy went a-fishing	J.C. Macey
Linden Lea	Vaughan Williams
Llwyn Onn (The Ash Grove)	arr. T.D. Jones
Myfanwy	Parry
Wrth gofio'r dyddiau gynt (Remembering Past Days)	arr. Caradog Roberts

'Madam Ivor Rees', my mother, was blessed with her father's sunny sense of humour, and I am sure that she would have been amused by the many different ways in which she was referred to in programmes, news articles and reviews of the time, but especially here, as the article in the newspaper immediately beneath her name boasted the headline, **'Visitor Praises Swansea's Pretty Girls'! Geoff Rees**

The choice of music, appropriately perhaps for a programme broadcast relatively late in the evening, is composed of beautifully peaceful, and nostalgic songs, descriptive of the healing powers of nature, of unfulfilled love and of longing for the past. The song-list also reflects the influence of Jack Newbury's earlier involvement in The Welsh Imperials, including as it does one lighter item by the prolific American composer J.C. Macey, and a closing, valedictory piece arranged by the highly regarded North Walian musician and composer Caradog Roberts.

Listening to this delightful collection of famous and less famous melodies, one cannot but be moved by the hindsight that The Swansea Imperials' promising and accomplished first broadcast came less than three weeks before September 3rd, 1939, when Neville Chamberlain was to make his momentous announcement that Britain was at war with Hitler's Germany.

Gradually, other excellent singers were to became involved with 'The Imperials' through the 'grapevine' of their membership of larger choirs. **John Hayward's father, Ernest, as previously mentioned, sang with the Swansea and District** and was amongst the earliest, most committed, and longest serving members of the Imperials.

Ernest, sang with the Swansea and District with a powerful, deep bass voice

One of the **older singers, with a powerful, deep bass voice,** 'Ern' had served in Mesopotamia during World War I, but when he returned from the army in 1919 to 'the land fit for heroes' and to his home town of Worcester, he found that jobs were very scarce.

Ern completed his apprenticeship as a coach painter but spent almost two years without work, all the time applying for jobs around the country. Eventually, he moved to Swansea in the early 1920s. That he and so many others were prepared to move so far from home for a tradesman's post is an indication of how tough times were. However, after one look at Swansea Bay and

Gower, he decided never to return to Worcester. Ern's son, John, says that his father came to love his adopted town dearly.

Ern found employment at Palmer and Evans, a motor body shop located in a lane adjacent to the old Swansea Hospital off Bryn-Y-Mor Road, and he remained working there for 48 years until the firm closed on his 70th birthday. It was the only job that he ever had.

Ern's first wife was also interested in singing and so they had their voices trained. Amusingly, he is said to have commented, tongue-in-cheek, that he also learned to sing in Welsh, while admitting that he never understood any of the words that he sang !

After the loss of his first wife, Ern married John's mother Alice, and the two continued singing at Argyle Chapel in St. Helen's Road in the centre of Swansea, which had a flourishing choir throughout this period. John recalls that his father used to reminisce about walking from his home in Francis Street to choir rehearsals with a police inspector friend – the walk in company and conversation through town was no trial to him, but just another part of his joyful association with the Imperials.

One needs only a quick glance at local papers in the **1930s to understand what a difficult period this was for the people of Swansea, which, like other parts of Britain and the World, was feeling the full onset of the Depression.** Apart from the stresses of work, there were persistent and virulent diseases, as yet uncured. Olive Rees lost her two sisters to polio and TB, while Ivor lost a younger sister during an outbreak of scarlet fever in 1942.

But in this time before television, people were wholly committed to providing entertainment for themselves to take their minds off the darker aspects of life. The Swansea Imperials performed in Churches and Chapels at Easter and at Christmas concerts, and were to quickly build a reputation for the purity of their singing and range of repertoire. However, their initial success and togetherness as a choir was now to be threatened by the sound of 'distant thunder' in Europe.

The **BBC Studios in Alexandra Road**, in the centre of Swansea, had only recently opened in October 1937, and the choir were quick to seize the opportunities that this offered to performers who lived in South West Wales.

(Photo courtesy of SW Evening Post)

Stave6

Imperials at War

('They gave their services unstintedly')

Premature warnings of the threat of Fascism in Europe were felt in Swansea as early as 1936

Premature warnings of the threat of Fascism in Europe were felt in Swansea as early as 1936 at the outbreak of the Spanish Civil War. Some principled local men sought to help by supporting the International Brigades and the other chaotic forces opposing General Franco, during a conflict in which his German ally, Hitler, perfected the devastating art of 'Blitzkreig'. Ern Hayward and his first wife provided board for a university student lodger each year. One idealistic young man, who had been staying with them, decided to join the desperate fight against Franco ... but never returned.

While the British Government adopted a policy of appeasing Hitler, the self-styled 'Fuerher' continued to pursue his grandiose ideas of bringing most of Germany's neighbouring countries under Nazi influence and of breaking every clause of the 1919 Treaty of Versailles.

A line in the sand seemed to have been drawn by an agreement reached between Prime Minister Chamberlain and Hitler at Munich in October 1938, only for the German leader to break his word and invade Czechoslovakia in the following Spring. Despite warnings, either because he did not believe or because he did not care that Britain and France would oppose him militarily, Hitler ordered the invasion of Poland by German forces in September 1939 and thus triggered the catastrophe of World War II.

1939

For most people in Great Britain, the declaration of war with Germany in September 1939 was alarming but not unexpected as a widespread feeling of anxiety and foreboding had gripped the nation for some time. In Swansea self-defence preparations had begun commendably early and yet, during the period known as **'The Phoney War'**, less than one would have expected seemed to be happening to disrupt normal life. Some far-off battles at sea affected the families of Swansea sailors, and local men joined the armed forces, but no immediate air-raids were experienced on the town which, it must be remembered, was still one of Britain's most significant ports at the time.

However, the late Spring of 1940 saw a serious escalation of the War as Hitler's panzer Divisions swept into Holland, Belgium. Norway, and France. By late May of that year, 350,000 British troops found themselves on the retreat and stranded on the beaches and in the ports of Northern France. Their miraculous rescue by a flotilla of large ships and small boats from the beach at Dunkirk and elsewhere has since become the stuff of legend.

One future member of the 'Imperials' who experienced at first hand the drama of this mass evacuation was Frank Newbury. In 1939 with a number of friends at work, Frank went to join up. Before going to the recruiting office they took advice from some First World War veterans who suggested the RAF as a more glamorous service. The recruiting officer had different ideas and Frank was signed up into the Royal Army Service Corps (now called the Royal Logistic Corps).

In early 1940, Frank was sent to Nantes in Western France where he was able to use his grammar school French. Although most have heard of the Dunkirk operation which took place from May 26th until 4th June 1940, it is not widely appreciated that the evacuation of British forces was also managed from several other ports in France a little later. Some members of Frank's unit were ordered to stay behind and destroy stores and equipment to prevent them falling into enemy hands. Frank and others were transported in train cattle-wagons to the port of St. Malo and they boarded one of the last ships to leave the mainland of Europe for Britain in late June.

1940

All seemed lost for the Allied cause .... but Frank and his comrades would return.

© Everett Collection Historica/Alamy Stock Photo

During August and September of 1940, the 'Battle of Britain' raged above Southern England as the Luftwaffe tried to eliminate the capability of the RAF. The heroic exploits of British and Allied pilots became immortalised forever in the words of **Britain's new War Leader, Winston Churchill:**

'Never in the field of human conflict was so much owed by so many to so few.'

Realising that he could not defeat the RAF, Hitler switched his strategy to trying to bomb Britain out of the War. The first heavy bombing raid on East London occurred on the night of 7th September and the German terror campaign soon spread to other British cities.

With American involvement in the war more than a year away, Britain stood alone, and the fear of invasion in those Autumn months seemed to be in everyone's mind.

The German capture of airports in Northern France and Holland brought Swansea within range of German bombers. In documents discovered since the war, it can be seen that the town had been identified by Hitler as a priority target, and air-raids and air-raid warnings became a part of everyday life for the population of Swansea.

The Rees family decided to take precautions.. In September 1940, my mother, Olive Rees, was due to give birth to my older brother Esmond. The threat of bombing raids was enough to make my parents take evasive action, and my mother was swiftly escorted to Torquay in Devon, as they believed a seaside holiday resort to be safer than a heavily industrialised town like Swansea. My mother stayed for a few weeks with her sister Muriel Davies, who had moved there with her railway worker husband, Emlyn, just before the war.

My much-loved, handsome brother, Philip Esmond Rees, was born in Torquay on 26th September and, after a few weeks, my mother returned to Wales. Esmond became a staunch Welshman but was often gently teased by our inner circle of family about his English origins!

Also in 1940, my parents moved from my grandparents' house in Cwmbwrla, which was near the strategically important Cwmfelin Steel and Tinplate Works and the industrial heartland of Swansea. They made their new home in Overland Road in the Mumbles, where they and their newly-born son shared a house divided into three flats. The other occupants were another family of three, and two sisters who were Sunday School teachers.
Geoff Rees

> The Luftwaffe's flight path to Liverpool took bombers directly over the town, and **Swansea sometimes became the unfortunate 'beneficiary' of any 'leftovers'** on the Germans' return journey.

Reginald Foort and the Swansea and District Royal Male-Voice Choir outside the Empire Theatre.

Remarkably, despite sporadic German attacks and the widespread anxiety and belief that Swansea would one day endure the kind of devastating raid that other cities had experienced, the people of the town continued about their daily working lives and pastimes. Cinemas, although initially closed on the declaration of war, remained open and some musical events carried on.

In October 1940, the celebrated organist, **Reginald Foort, (reputedly the most popular musician in Britain at the time) visited Swansea on a national morale-building tour.** Ivor's autographed photo, taken outside The Empire Theatre, features the artiste with the Swansea and District choir. The picture includes several other men who were to join the Swansea Imperials including Ern Hayward who can be seen second right. Ivor Rees is standing centrally, directly under the Capstan sign while Reginald Foort is fifth from the left next to conductor Ivor Owen. The choir had been contracted to sing throughout the second week of Reginald's presence at the Empire, which once stood proudly next door to the building that these days is occupied by Waterstone's Bookshop in Oxford Street.

Public morale was boosted by concerts such as these and every effort was made to keep cinemas and theatres open, not only as a source of information but to offer an emotional uplift in these deeply worrying times.

However, Swansea was changing for all to see, and one diarist recorded that the sea-front had gradually become almost unrecognisable.

'Surprising how easily one can get used to war conditions. Barrage balloons in the sky, military cars and soldiers, guns in the fields, strong points in house walls and on the roadside, stakes set up in the bays, and anti-tank blocks along the shore and inland, do not even draw a glance.'

(from 'The Swansea Wartime Diary of Laurie Latchford)

To date, we have not discovered any evidence of concerts by the Swansea Imperials during the early days of the war, but, knowing their resilience as a group of dedicated musicians, we feel sure that they would have tried to continue. Even so, public gatherings were considered unsafe, air-raids and the threat of air-raids on Swansea were increasing and rehearsals became difficult to organise. Ivor Rees, for instance, was now faced with a ten mile drive to and from Swansea, sometimes in total darkness due to the blackout. Geoff believes that during one pitch-black evening, another driver drove into the car that was his father's pride and joy, writing it off.

The ICI Works was given over to the war effort and men were working extra hours. In the old Upper Bank Works, on the site of the more recent Addis Factory, and just across the road from the present-day Swansea. com Stadium, the government had for some years been preparing a factory to produce ammunition and shells for battleships. **Ivor Rees was transferred to 'QF' (the 'Quick Firing Factory')**, further distancing him from some of his friends and singing comrades. This was an extremely dangerous posting, but, happily, despite their desperation to find and destroy 'QF', the Luftwaffe don't seem to have managed a direct strike, apart from one solitary incendiary bomb. (for an excellent description of work at QF see Felicity's Kilpatrick's 'Down the Memory lanes of My Hafod').

German aircraft may have missed many of their military targets but their escalating attacks were soon to have a devastating effect on the town of our mothers and fathers. In January **1941, bombs landed in the Cwm area below Waun Wen, near to the Cwmfelin Works**, killing many civilians and their children. This tragedy, however, was only a foretaste of the destruction that was to follow.

Stave 7

The Three Nights' Blitz

The "Three Nights Blitz" turned the town into a terrifying inferno

During three nights of concentrated bombing on 19th, 20th and 21st of February 1941, the central shopping area of Swansea was completely decimated.

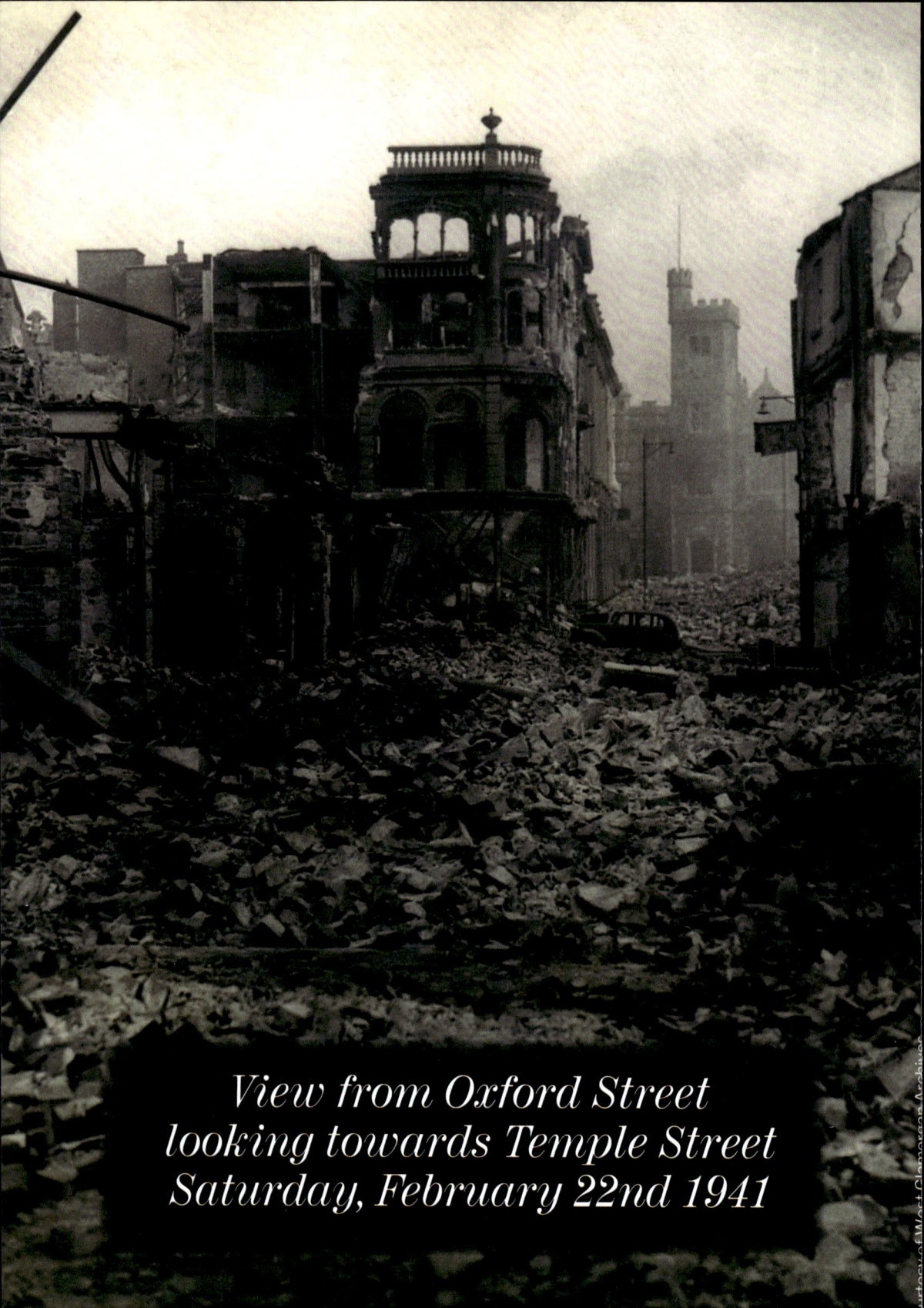

*View from Oxford Street
looking towards Temple Street
Saturday, February 22nd 1941*

The 'Three Nights Blitz' turned the town into a terrifying inferno and reduced it to a desert of swirling ash and smouldering rubble.

The beautiful ornate Ben Evans

My father, like all the other men and women featured in this book, loved pre-war Swansea. As I grew up I would hear anyone of his generation say the same. The town centre had been a bustling, bright and wonderful place for the people of South West Wales to enjoy. At the heart of it had sat the magnificent Ben Evans department store which sold everything under the sun – it was absolutely the 'Harrods' or 'Selfridges' of Wales. My mother's older sister, Muriel, had been a shop assistant at Ben Evans' after leaving school – to have such a position was to be considered amongst the crème-de-la-crème of shop-workers. **Geoff Rees**

The store was more than just a shop, housing as it did young apprentices who wished to learn dressmaking and tailoring skills and even catering for their souls with Sunday services held in the building. This landmark business, with its beautiful, ornate facade and distinctive cupola was razed to the ground, never to be replaced. After the war the land was turned into gardens. Today the site is an open, paved, public space – Castle Square.

In his 1947 broadcast 'Return Journey', Dylan Thomas mourned the destruction of what had once been his 'sea-town world', where he had famously planned his creative future with other talented friends. They have since become known as the 'Kardomah Gang', after the cafe of that name in Castle Street where they met.

'I went out into the snow and walked down High Street past the flat white wastes where all the shops had been ... all the shops bombed and vanished ... '

In later years, Geoff's conversations with his father often led Ivor to say that the bombing had destroyed the cherished memories of his youth, just like they had for Dylan.

'On our excursions by bus into town in the mid 1950s, when I was a small boy, I would see the beginnings of new buildings, while Ivor, my father, would see only the ghosts of the old.'

Crucially, one of the buildings which was also severely damaged was the BBC Studio, where the Imperials had made their first recording.

In his story **'Extraordinary Little Cough'**, Dylan Thomas describes one of the girls that he meets as **'a distinguished piece and ..., as immaculate and unapproachable as a girl in Ben Evans' stores'.**

Geoff Rees

On free nights during wartime, both Ern Hayward and Ivor Rees served with the Home Guard.
For Olive Rees, relatively safe in the flat in the Mumbles overlooking Underhill Park, the most alarming noise was that of the ack-ack gun perched up on the hill at Thistleboon ... but on those terrible nights of the **'Three Nights Blitz'** across the bay, she too witnessed those pitiless fires of destruction and feared for the lives of her parents. Thankfully, my lovely grandparents, Will and Ruth Jenkins survived unscathed.

John Hayward tells the story of his father's participation in civil defence on the Home Front:

'By 1939 my father, Ern, was living in Francis Street, adjacent to the Guildhall and Victoria Park.
He was too old and short-sighted for the army, and so he joined the Swansea Home Guard. I do not have any of his wartime stories that can be pin-pointed to the **'Three Nights Blitz'**, but I know he was on duty with his platoon in the town centre. The Home Guard's primary responsibility was to prevent looting.

He told me that they were allowed to carry loaded guns when on duty, unlike the regular army on home soil. He also told me that they were instructed to shoot looters who refused to stop on command, though, thankfully, they never shot anyone. Their other main duties during the war included manning the anti-aircraft guns in the Mumbles.

The Home Guard were equipped with live ammunition but they did not get any at first. When finally the ammunition did arrive, it needed to be marked with the platoon identifiers. As my father was a coach painter, it was agreed to have the ammunition delivered to his house and stored in the front room where he painted the markings. He often reflected on what would have happened if a bomb had landed nearby.

Ern Hayward with his Swansea Home Guard Unit

One night, an incendiary bomb did hit the shed in the back garden but it did not ignite, and my father covered it with sandbags until some 'official' was able to deal with it.

He told me that a large unexploded bomb had landed near the old Swansea Hospital, perhaps in Hospital Square itself (possibly on the night of 16th February, 1943). The area was cleared and a bomb disposal officer tried to deal with it. Sadly, the bomb exploded and the officer lost his life. A sobering experience was in store for my father when he met a policeman the following day who was searching amongst the debris for the remains of this very brave man.

On another occasion, one of my father's fellow Home Guard soldiers called at the house saying there was an alert of an imminent German invasion and that the Home Guard were to gather immediately near the seashore.

Typically unruffled, my father and his comrade decided to have a cup of tea first, ... consider the situation ...., and only then go down to the meeting place. There was no invasion.'

John also relates, 'My older half-sister, Barbara, who has helped in the writing of this book, was in school during the first part of the war, before, along with many others, she was evacuated to Cardiganshire.'

Phil Newbury takes up the story:

In his evenings, **Jack Newbury** was a member of the ARP service (Air Raid Precautions). As a warden, he was required to establish a look-out post, usually on the Graig, Morriston, which was a high vantage point affording panoramic views of the east of Swansea and the Lower Swansea Valley. During air-raids, wardens would be looking for and reporting on areas of the town and its outskirts which were ablaze.

Mindful then that his role was to protect civilians from the dangers of air-raids, it was ironic that Jack, on returning home during a heavy bombing raid, went straight to check the basement shelter under his mother-in-law's house next door.

'Not finding my mother, Carrie, there, my father immediately rushed next door, only to find her lying under their bed, calmly reading a book and enjoying a cigarette! Swiftly, he seized her legs and dragged her out and they both rushed to the safety of the shelter, joining the rest of the extended family.'

Swansea was bombed more intensively and lost more lives than anywhere else in Wales during the Nazi air-raids.

Since the end of 1941, the RAF had placed a contingent of fighter planes and airmen at Fairwood and German attackers saw the runway and buildings as a fair military target. However, such was the inaccuracy of bombers, the enemy managed only a strike on an outhouse cabin that comprised the Waafs' living quarters.

The last attack from the skies came on the evening of 16th February, 1943, which tragically took the lives of

34 people,

including three casualties at Fairwood Aerodrome.

Tragically, three vivacious, young women who were on site at Fairwood were killed.

"A close cricketing friend has recently told me that his mother had been based at the aerodrome. It had been her night off, and she had gone into Swansea to meet friends, thus miraculously escaping the terrible fate of her comrades."

The Fairwood air crews pursued the Luftwaffe planes on that night, wounding one and forcing it to ditch in the sea, just off the Gower Coast. Another was severely damaged and, although the four airmen on board made it across the Bristol Channel, their plane crashed into farm buildings in the Dorset countryside. The events of that fateful night are the subject of R.T. Pearce's excellent **'Operation Wasservogel'** in which the author traces the lives, not only of the young Waafs and RAF pilots, but also of their dead German counterparts, all of them seemingly decent men with promising lives before them. **Such is the senseless waste of war.**

Stave 8

American invasion

The devastating Japanese attack on the American naval base at Pearl Harbor in the Pacific

December 1941

© Dom Slike/Alamy Stock Photo

The devastating Japanese attack on the American naval base at Pearl Harbor in thc Pacific in December 1941 brought the United States into the war on the side of the Allies. In late 1943, early 1944, American soldiers began to arrive in South West Wales in their thousands – some billeted with the public, but the majority based in big camps around the Swansea area at Mumbles, Bishopston, the Racecourse in Manselton, Ashleigh Road, Clasemont, Penllergaer Woods and Scurlage in South Gower.

The Americans came with little booklets encouraging them to be kind and generous to their British hosts. They even organised a concert, and an American Football game at St. Helen's during which the most severely injured casualty was the referee who ended up in Morriston Hospital!

© Stephen Barnes/Military / Alamy Stock Photo

1942

British and American servicemen drink a toast, 1942.

'And suddenly they were all around us, in the dances, in the parks, on the buses, testing their jeeps on the Hafod tips. One regiment with an Indian Chief's head for an emblem even raised a totem pole on the hill above Morriston Hospital... A handsome, generous young man was billeted with a family in our street and was always bringing them provisions and giving out gum and chocolate for the kids. I often wonder what happened to him...' **(School project 2000)**

Perhaps the most celebrated visitor to Swansea from the across the Atlantic was an as yet unknown private from Brockton named **Rocco Francis Marchegiano**. As legend would have it, Rocco, based in Swansea from December 1943, developed a taste for fish and chips and even the local seaweed speciality laverbread. However, in his letters to his family, he revealed his shock at how deprived the locals were compared with folk back home.

'Food was being rationed and my father, Ivor, recalled frequently being asked to entertain the drinkers in a local public house and sing for the reward of a few eggs or some fruit from the landlord.'

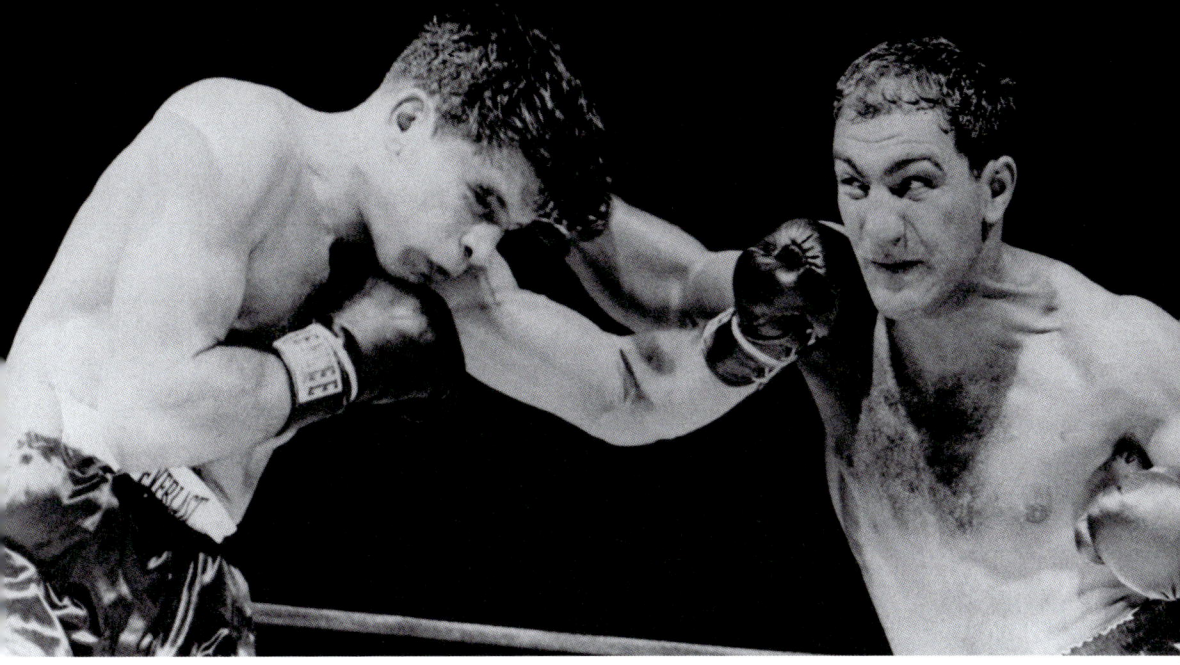

The most famous story about Rocco also took place in a hostelry. One night at the Adelphi pub in Wind Street in the town centre, Rocco and a few friends got into a heated argument with a tall Australian soldier. The much smaller Rocco settled the row, as he would do so often in his later boxing career, with one explosive punch to the jaw which knocked the much bigger man out, ... **for 'Rocco' was to be the future 'Rocky Marciano'**, who became in the 1950s the Heavyweight Champion of the World, and who remained undefeated throughout his professional career.

This was not the only scrape that Rocky got himself into and, as part of his punishment, his superiors suggested that he concentrate his energies on the discipline of boxing training at Jimmy Wilde's gym near Swansea's High Street Railway Station. This tactic does not seem to have curbed his temper in the long run, however, as Rocky never actually made it across the Channel to face the Germans, having become involved in a further incident just before his unit left Weymouth in Mid June 1944.

Roland La Starza lands a left on the chin of **Rocky Marciano**, 1953.

Some of the preparations for the Allied assault on the coast of Normandy had taken place on the beautiful beaches of Gower.

'I'll never forget the endless procession of armoured vehicles that rumbled and roared through Cockett and away down to Swansea. Even as a young boy I knew that some great battle was about to take place.'
(school project 2000)

Ivor Rees recalled the massed ranks of boats of all sizes which had been gathered into Swansea Bay to convey the soldiers and equipment to the beaches in Normandy. **He once told Geoff,** 'There were so many vessels that you could have run right across the breadth of the Bay without once getting your feet wet!'

On 'D-Day', June 6th, the Allies launched 'Operation Overlord' their decisive invasion of Northern France.

1944

'*I recently stood at the end of Overland Road, which overlooks the Bay and imagined the unforgettable sight of that small armada which lay before him in the lead-up to the D-Day landings.*

'*Operation Overlord' was to be the campaign that changed the course of World History as American, Canadian, British and Allied troops risked their lives to free Europe from the 'tyranny' of Nazi occupation'*

Geoff Rees

Frank   *Jack*

'Music played a great part in Frank's smooth return to civilian life, in particular, performing alongside his brother, Jack, in **The Swansea Imperial Singers.**'

Elsewhere, **Frank Newbury, on his return from France, had been sent for officer training, and, shortly afterwards, was commissioned**. His nephew, Brinley writes, 'Towards the end of 1942 he was sent to another front, and an already secured port in North Africa. As an officer he stepped off his ship without his kit which would have been brought ashore later. However, just at this moment, an enemy plane passed over and dropped a bomb which scored a direct hit on the ship and sank it! **Frank would remark,**

'*All I had were the clothes I stood up in.*'

His expensive spare uniform, hand-tailored at local Swansea men's outfitters, 'Sidney Heath', lay at the bottom of the sea!

Frank later joined the Allied invasion of Italy and served in Greece before returning home and being demobbed. Although he witnessed many horrible incidents in the war in terms of loss of life, mutilation and depravity, these were things of which he never spoke, but rather he took from his experiences a positive outlook on life and a desire to make the most of future opportunities. It was not easy for him returning to **'civvy street'** after the war and trying to regain a sense of normality.'

While many forms of entertainment from soccer to theatre to singing were disrupted by the war with Nazi Germany, there was one medium of the arts which came into its own – the **Radio. One of the BBC's most successful programmes, 'ITMA' or 'It's That Man Again'**, starring Tommy Handley was actually recorded and transmitted from Bangor in North Wales while the Blitz continued over London. It must have seemed ironic to the programme-makers in South Wales that such a tremendously popular programme was being produced in the North without any tinge of 'Welshness' to it, and it is likely that it was this that provoked them to design their own home-based show to compete with their English rivals.

That programme was named **'Welsh Rarebit'** and it began life as a Forces' feature designed for the entertainment of homesick servicemen. Even so, it soon became very popular and was included from time to time in the schedule of the Home Service. Although it was chiefly a variety show, it had regular items which included

1st July
1944

© SuperStock/Alamy Stock Photo

Eynon Evans playing the hapless **'Tommy Troubles'**. The programme gave work to many Welsh entertainers such as Gladys Morgan and Wyn Calvin, and offered a springboard to young and up and coming stars like Harry Secombe and Stan Stennett who were returning from the War, and who were to become household names.

The programme's inspirational director and conductor was the talented musician Mai Jones who, with Lyn Joshua, also composed the famous closing music to the show .... **'They'll keep a Welcome in the Hillsides ...'** The programme ended in 1944 but returned on **St. David's Day after the war, running as a weekly show until the early 1950s, and, as we shall see, it was to play a memorable part in the story of the Swansea Imperials.**

Tommy Handley entertains the Navy. He arrives at a railway station to travel, with the rest of the "ITMA" Company, to a Naval Base, for a week of concerts including the regular **"ITMA" programme in the BBC home service on January 13.**

Stave 9

'Radio fun'

1947

After six years of tear and destruction, and disruption to their everyday lives, the **Swansea Imperials under the leadership of Jack Newbury emerged phoenix-like from those dark years, as a choir of outstanding ability and excellent quality.** However, they were no longer the 'Octet' of 1938 but a tightly-knit, beautifully balanced choir of 17 men, drawn from widely separated districts of Swansea – from Morriston to Mumbles, from Townhill to Brynmill and Sketty.

A 'Herald of Wales' report from February 1947, states that,

The classic post-war photo of the **Swansea Imperial Singers**.

'During the war years, they (The Imperials) gave their services unstintedly in aid of all kinds of war efforts and local charities, to the troops at various gun-sites and in most of the local emergency hospitals.'

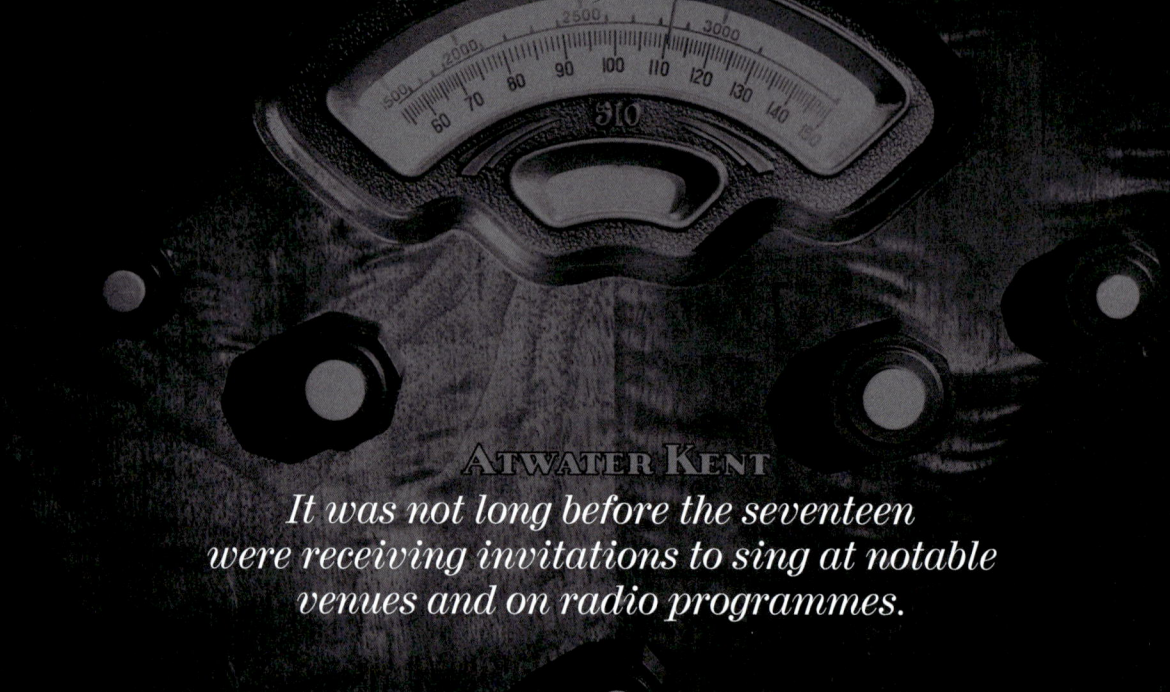

ATWATER KENT

It was not long before the seventeen
were receiving invitations to sing at notable
venues and on radio programmes.

I have vague memories of my parents saying that they had met some ENSA performers and played in concerts near the local troop camps, but with none of the Imperials still alive, how the choir grew in size is down to pure speculation. The Swansea and District Choir were still performing under Ivor Owen during the war and these gatherings may have been the moments when invitations were passed on. This may also have been the case in that hotbed of choral singing, Morriston, where Jack and Tal were living.

Geoff Rees

Newspapers in 1946 were referring to the heartfelt desire of the nation to return to 'normality' and there can be no doubting that the singers wished to restore a degree of beauty, harmony and joy to their lives.
There were still hardships to overcome in the immediate post-war years, in the form of rationing and the terrible winter months at the beginning of 1947, but it was not long before the seventeen were receiving invitations to sing at notable venues and on radio programmes.

Outstanding amongst a number of successful concert engagements were those at the King's Hall in Aberystwyth, the Music and Arts Club, Milford Haven, and at the Grand Pavilion, Porthcawl.

The Porthcawl concert performed on Sunday 30th September, just six weeks after the end of the war in the Far East, inspired the following review in **'the Glamorgan Gazette' on the 5th October:**

'The Swansea Imperial Singers gave an excellent concert at the Grand Pavilion .... under the conductorship of Jack Newbury. Supporting artists were Madame L.M. Wilkins (soprano), Miss Pat Kern (contralto), Madame Frances Matthews (elocutionist) ... and the accompanist was Miss Olive Rees R.A.M. Mr C. Hughes Davies was at the electric organ.'

One can only imagine the sense of release and exhilaration that the choir must have felt after the restrictions of the war years.

It is great credit to the ability of their leader Jack Newbury and to the quality of the Imperials that the core of the choir could just pick up from where they were before the War and that others were inspired to enrol and join them in song.

Jack lived and breathed for his choir and would often shut himself away in the family front room after dinner, selecting a programme of work, transposing, notating and arranging the many individual parts to suit the different male voices.
Jack's son, Phil says,

'No two concerts would be the same. The selection of music would be adapted to suit the audience and venue, whether it be churches, chapels, old peoples' homes, working men's clubs or ... for broadcasting.'

The Swansea Imperial Singers: Their next event— all-star concert

THE Swansea Imperial Singers, under the able leadership of Mr. Jack Newbury have come well to the fore in Swansea musical circles as a choir of outstanding ability and excellent quality.

Mr. Newbury himself is a well-known bass vocalist who some years ago toured Britain, America and Canada with the former Welsh Imperial Singers, a choir composed of singers selected from all parts of the country. Formed in 1938, the Swansea Imperial Singers were originally known as and ...

Back row: H.S. Evans (Organising Secretary), A. Edwards, B. Davies, G. Bevan, J. H. Dennis, E. Richards, E. Morgan, E. Hayward, and T. Griffiths.
Front row: G. Owen, T. Horne, B. Williams, I. Rees, Madam Olive Rees, Jack Newbury, D. Greaves, J. Bainbridge and W. James.

Photograph of the **Imperials from February 22nd 1947**. 'Herald of Wales'

Ken Williams

After being demobbed, Frank Newbury returned to his work at the Post Office and joined his brother's thriving choir, and there were other outstanding alterations to this line-up such as Ken Williams, who had served in the tank corps during the War.
Ken's nephew, Colin Williams writes,

'My father's brother Ken, an outstanding tenor, was a member of the Imperials for some time. After the choir disbanded he was 'head-hunted' by Ivor Sims to join the Morriston Orpheus during the 'halcyon years'. Ken went on to become for many years the chief tenor soloist of the Orpheus and can be heard on their wonderful recording of 'Hiraeth'
Ken Williams

As the Imperials' fame spread east of Cardiff, at the end of 1946, the choir received an offer from the Gaumont State Cinema, Kilburn London – one of the largest movie-houses in Great Britain – for twice-nightly performances for one week. At this time it was not unusual for cinemas to present concerts and for theatres to present movies.

Unfortunately, as all the members of the choir were working men, it was found impossible to accept this engagement, which was the more disappointing because that particular week royalty visited the cinema on two occasions. It is likely that Jack may not have wanted to be too far from home as his son Phil, was born at the beginning of January 1947.

The choir was also engaged to sing in an all-star concert at the Swansea Empire Theatre on March 9th in aid of the Swansea Hospital and St. John Ambulance Association. Over the next decade the Imperials raised thousands of pounds for local charities. The President of the choir was Hugh Cann MBE who had sung with the Swansea and District Choir, and knew many of the Imperials well. His connection with the choir is almost certainly why Singleton Hospital figured so highly in their list of charitable beneficiaries as he was Commissioner in Swansea for the Order of St. John of Jerusalem.

Hugh retired in 1945 after 50 years' service to education in Swansea, latterly as Chief Assistant to the Director of Education. He had received the MBE for his wartime work when he was seconded to be organiser of 'communal and school feeding' in Swansea.

During late February and March 1941, over 25 thousand cooked meals were served to the homeless, rescue services and displaced families. Two British restaurants, started at short notice, were the first in Wales.

The test of Hugh's organisational skills came during the **Three Nights' Blitz** when, on one single day, over

2000 people, were fed with soup of fresh meat and vegetables at the 17 centres he had established.

On Tuesday, 17th June 1947, the choir began a series of radio recordings stretching over the next decade with 'Sing a Song of Sunshine', an appropriately named programme if ever there was one.
The item was broadcast on the Light programme at 10.00 a.m, following on immediately after the very popular 'Housewives' Choice'. The cast included Zoe Cresswell (soprano), Rita Smart and Eileen Davies ('2 pianos') and of course, 'The Swansea Imperial Singers', conductor Jack Newbury (soloist John Morgan).

This must have been a success, for shortly afterwards in December of the same year, the choir was granted its own half-hour programme on the Welsh Home Service, possibly recorded at the substitute studios in a school room in Grove Place or at the Ragged School in Pleasant Street, both of these venues close to where the ruins of the Swansea BBC Studios stood in Alexandra Road.

In July 1948, once again on the Home Service, The Imperials showed their versatility in a programme with the BBC Welsh Orchestra entitled 'From the Operas'.

'The Evening Post' reported

'The Swansea Imperial Singers, under their conductor, Mr Jack Newbury, are in great demand these days and tonight they are again broadcasting various items from operatic music, accompanied by the BBC Welsh Orchestra, conducted by Mr Mansel Thomas.

'The Evening Post' article mentions the 'many' performances that the choir had already made for radio. Some of these are traceable through old copies of 'The Radio Times', but programmes on the Welsh Home Service, particularly after the War, are not recorded in such detail with a full cast list.

The Programme includes items from
'Rigoletto', 'The Magic Flute', etc.
This fine combination has already been
on the air on many occasions and at
a recent rehearsal Mr Mansel Thomas
complimented the choir on its fine
singing and its originality in choice
of pieces. The accompanist at
all the concerts and broadcasts is
Madam Olive Rees.'

In this same month the Singers gave a concert in Borth, near Aberystwyth where they were treated like celebrities and with great hospitality.

The range of the choir at this time seemed infinite, from light entertainment, to traditional Welsh songs, and to the high drama of these operatic pieces. We have read of Jack Newbury's complete mastery of difficult arias from Mozart while a member of the Welsh Imperials, but all of his Swansea choir had their own small portfolio of items. "I can recall at home my father, Ivor Rees, practising 'The Flower Song' from 'Carmen' and several of the tenor solos which he loved from Puccini's operas – 'la Boheme', 'Tosca' and 'Turandot'. His favourite operatic piece was the duet from 'The Pearl Fishers' by Bizet."

My mother also could often be heard playing the introduction to an aria from Leoncavallo's 'Pagliacci' and the intermezzo from 'Cavalleria Rusticana'. All of these works were within the capabilities of the choir. Some of the beautiful melodies became so fixed in my mind as a youngster that, when I left home for University in 1969, one of the first long-playing records that I bought (after 'Abbey Road') was an anthology of famous voices from the operas.'
Geoff Rees

After extensive research, a small article from December, 1948 finally revealed the extent of the choir's activities and impressive organisation:

The Imperials at one of their Christmas concerts

It was reported that the choir had had a very successful year, taking part in eight broadcasts and more than

20 concerts.
(SW Evening Post)

The Officers elected for 1949 were:

President: Mr Hugh Cann MBE

Chairman: Mr Walter James (retiring)

Conductor: Mr Jack Newbury

Accompanist: Madame Olive Rees

Treasurer: Mr Ernest Hayward

Minute Secretary: Mr Ivor Rees

Hon. Secretary: Mr Alwyn Edwards

Librarian: Mr Tommy Horn

Chairman for 1949: Mr Edgar Richards

It is clear that by 1948 the Imperials were being run along professional lines and by a very able, committed and loyal team of choir members.

"During that year, my parents and brother moved from Mumbles to a flat above a painting and decorating shop at 51, St. Helen's Road near Swansea's town centre, which had been so badly damaged in the War. However, the road had emerged from the Blitz remarkably unscathed. The shop was managed by Adelina Williams who lived nearby in Christina Street. She was a very kind elderly lady, and was known affectionately to me and my brother as 'Auntie Addie'. When I was born in 1951 she became like another grandmother to me. The other flat in the building was occupied by the Jeremy family, and their daughter Judith, who for the short time we knew one another, treated me like her little baby brother.

The flat was located almost equidistantly between Swansea Town's famous Vetch Field and the equally famous St. Helen's Cricket and Football Ground. In the fine summer of 1948 my father was able to take my seven years old brother to see the last few hours of several Glamorgan games as the team won the County Championship for the first time, under the captaincy of Wilf Wooler, recording 13 victories. The move was also the beginning of our family's love affair with the Swans, who, over the next decade, began to produce some of the finest home-bred players in the history of Welsh football."
Geoff Rees

"My mother and father could both read music like several others in the choir, but as one correspondent to 'The Western Mail' commented at this time, in his opinion '95% of male-voice choir members' used not classical musical notation but 'sol-fa'. Adapting copies for the choir from the original must have been very time-consuming for Jack. Classical notation is a very skilled art, and if a song has been originally written in an unusual key, the positioning of notes and chords on the stave can become bewildering to the untrained eye."
Geoff Rees

Stave10

A special year

Photo courtesy of The Evening Post

In the picture, the choir are standing in what appears to be High Street Station on their way to ...... where? Although Geoff's parents had kept the photo, they had also cut the caption off the bottom!

Eventually, two pieces of detective work solved the mystery. The first was a superb 'spot' by John Hayward. By careful analysis of the Decca Company's recording history, John was able to suggest that the choir may have made their four double-sided, wax records in London at the beginning of 1950. The second was the result of a microscopic search of information on the rear of the cutting which revealed the sale of a piece of real estate in a nearby village in January of that year.

A rapid search of 'The Post's' back numbers revealed the following front page item!

For many months during our research for this book one **'Evening Post' photograph of the choir defied dating and identification**.

Evening Post

No. 23,889   MONDAY, JANUARY 16, 1950   THREE-HALFPENCE

in gave £2,250,000,000 to   Swansea choir in London   Sm

in nations
N ON NEED
MONWEALTH
MIC UNITY

n Secretary, said to-day in
he has been attending the con-
ealth Foreign Ministers, that
ad contributed £750,000,000 in
from sterling balances to South
This was half the total post-war
million, of similar assistance
ther countries. The Common-
to grips, as it must do, with the
m.

THE WEATHER FORECAST

WALES: Moderate to fresh
northwesterly winds, showers
and fair periods. Rather cold
with ground and slight air
frost in sheltered places tonight.

TW
P
A s a
du
and So
of No.
sonienc
reduced
of pay

The Imperials were on their way to fulfil important engagements in the British capital, including recordings made for Decca. In addition, they took part on the Saturday night BBC Radio feature, 'In Town Tonight'. Kneeling in front are Jack Newbury, the conductor (left), and next to him Alwyn Edwards, the organising secretary.

The Imperials had indeed been to the recording studios, and, later in the day, found themselves being interviewed on BBC Radio's famous live Saturday evening programme while they were out and about in London. 'In Town Tonight' was broadcast from the British Capital and was another morale-boosting tonic for the nation. It consisted of roving reporters such as Brian Johnston interviewing passers-by at various famous places such as Piccadilly Circus, Oxford Circus and Trafalgar Square, as well as at the studios. **As Geoff comments**

How fantastic it would be to hear what was said that night. My parents, like many of the others, would have been very excited to have been walking amongst the bright lights of the West End, even though the city would have still shown the heavy ravages of war.
To my knowledge, they never ventured that far away from home again until my wedding in 1973.

Alas, no recording or transcript of the programme exists. A detailed analysis of the records made on that weekend follows in a later chapter of this book.

Just a couple of weeks later, on the first day of February, the choir were supporting artists in a half-hour radio review by ex-college friends, Brian Evans and Ronald Cass, called 'Come to the Fair' which was composed of comedy sketches and musical skits all set in a fairground. One sketch consisted of a rhymed commentary on a bout in a boxing booth ! Albeit that one of the scriptwriters worked for 'The Western Mail', the newspaper deemed the programme a 'triumph in light-heartedness'.

1950 perhaps found the choir at the peak of their powers. The year soon brought a flurry of invitations to participate in high profile radio programmes. The first of these very popular programmes was 'The George Mitchell Glee Club', and was recorded in front of a live audience at Swansea's famous Brangwyn Hall, before being broadcast on the Light Programme, right across the British Isles, just before Easter on Thursday 6th April at 8.30 p.m.

In 1950, **Radio, or 'wireless',** as our parents referred to it, **was still 'King'.**

'THE RADIO TIMES' FULL LISTING READS:

First in the series of 1950 with
The Mitchell Men
The Mitchell Maids
The George Mitchell Choir
'The Glee Club Sextet' led by Harold Smart
Solo Singers: Barbara Hope, James Charlton, Griff Griffiths, and Nickie Salisbury.
Tonight's guests are: 'The Swansea Imperial Singers', conductor Jack Newbury.
Master of Ceremonies: Leslie Mitchell. Produced by Dennis Main Wilson.

The Goon Show

© ZUMA Press, Inc./ Alamy Stock Photo

'The Glee Club' was broadcast weekly from venues all over Britain. Both George Mitchell and Dennis Main Wilson were to bridge the gap seamlessly into television broadcasting. Wilson, in particular, has been described as 'arguably the most important and influential of all comedy producers and directors in British radio and television'. His name was to appear at the foot of the credits on some of the most iconic programmes of all time – 'Hancock's Half Hour', 'The Goon Show', 'Sykes', 'The Rag Trade', 'Til Death Do Us Part', and 'Citizen Smith', to name but a few. He is also said to have given 'breaks' to Johnny Sullivan, Stephen Fry and Hugh Laurie, Griff Rhys Jones and Emma Thompson. He was a very gregarious down-to-earth and approachable man.

Both of my parents enjoyed his entertaining, natural, light-hearted company in the reception after the programme.
Geoff Rees

A transcript does still exist of this programme and reveals the high standards and discipline of all its top-class performers. 'Glee Club' was recorded on the Sunday prior to its broadcast, and rehearsals were held throughout the afternoon from 3.00 p.m. A complete run through took place from 6.30, before the warm-up at 7.50pm

'Glee Club' was a programme packed with all sorts of song – from romantic ballads like 'Only Make-Believe' and 'The Way You look Tonight', to children's favourites like 'The Teddy Bears' Picnic' ! It was a joyful and continuous stream of well- known music, and the full-house audience, packed with family members and friends of the choir, were encouraged to sing along at times to numbers like 'Enjoy Yourself' and 'Just a Song at Twilight'. **With Leslie Mitchell, the famous BBC and Movietone News commentator acting as Master of Ceremonies**, the programme was a model of timing and slickness, and an object lesson in presentation. Above all, it was the best of antidotes to the austere times in which **'The Imperials' were living ...**

'In times of worry, trouble, income tax and what-have-you, the best thing to do is to sing your head off!'

Picture Page television magazine programme seen here being broadcast from the BBC Studios at Alexandra Palace. **Leslie Mitchell, presenter off camera** here interviewing one of the guests in the studio.

Olive Rees, is dressed very glamorously for the evening.

Leslie Mitchell was stunned by the 'majestic' beauty of the hall, its surrounding walls adorned with the exotic Brangwyn panels.

When it came to the Imperials' time to sing, he had this to say:

"We couldn't have wished for a better place to start our Club series than here in the traditional land of song..... With us this evening are 'The Swansea Imperial Singers' – 17 male voices led by their conductor, Jack Newbury. They started life as an octet in 1938 during lunch-hour breaks at a local factory.

They now have 36 broadcasts to their credit – 37 tonight – and two months ago recorded 10 Welsh airs for one of the big recording companies in London.

In addition to all this, they have earned many thousands of pounds for charities – a fine record, isn't it? For their first song – well, it's one of the most moving of all Welsh airs – no programme with a Welsh choir would be complete without it – 'Ar Hyd Y Nos' – 'All through the Night'

Their performance was met with rapturous applause.

Later in the programme the choir sang 'Cyfrir Geifa' or 'Counting the Goats'. Again, Leslie Mitchell introduced and explained the song so eloquently and intelligibly,

This is 'an old traditional air from the Welsh mountains. It tells of a shepherd trying to count the goats in his flock – some white, some red, some blue – they move about so quickly that he can't keep up with them!'

At the end of the evening the programme concluded with an explosion of merriment and inspired community singing that in the opinion of one witness, 'brought the house down'. Everyone, including the George Mitchell Singers, sang 'Calon Lan' and 'Auld Lang Syne together.

'The Evening Post' reported
'When listeners tune in to the George Mitchell Glee Club ..... they will hear half-an-hour of excellent entertainment ... The guests were the Swansea Imperial Singers conducted by Jack Newbury, and both Leslie Mitchell and the George Mitchell Choir were genuinely impressed with their performance.

Just reading the transcript of the programme one becomes intoxicated with the atmosphere and **excitement of that splendid night in the lives of the choir.**

('Sut Hwyl'.
'The Imperial Singers are seen in the background at the recording in the Ragged School. In the foreground are John Griffiths, producer, Harriet Lewis, George David, Dylis Davies and Gunstone Jones, the 'regulars' of the programme.)

A few weeks after the prestigious Brangwyn Hall concert, on May 1st, the Imperials were performing and recording for the popular Welsh Language programme, 'Sut Hwyl'. This was an episode from another light entertainment series, which combined comedy sketches with song, and had served as a morale-boosting Forces' Broadcast during the War. It had developed from an earlier version of the programme in the 1930s, which had been simply named 'Hwyl' .

After the destruction of its Swansea base in 1941, the programme relocated its recordings to Carmarthen before moving back to Swansea in December 1947. **'Sut Hwyl' that evening in 1950 was recorded at the Swansea Ragged School**, situated near the old police Station in Pleasant Street, one of the few buildings in that area of the town centre not to have been demolished by the Luftwaffe in February 1941.

They were followed by their devoted flock
of family members and admiring friends

1950

The surroundings may have been less elevated than the Brangwyn Hall but illustrate again the reliability and flexibility of the choir. They were in demand and would always turn up at the top of their game.

Less than a fortnight later, The Swansea Imperials made their debut in 'Welsh Rarebit'. This programme at its height was said to have had nearly 12 million listeners.

"One of my mother's favourite phrases was

'little and good', used often to describe members of her parents' family who were all under 5 feet four.'

Wherever they travelled the Singers were followed by their devoted flock of family members and admiring friends. Jack Newbury is front row nursing his son Phil, while Ivor Rees, is centre front row and holding Geoff's 10 years old brother Esmond. Ern Hayward is standing in the very back row, second from the left.

1950

It's not surprising then that Olive's favourite artiste from 'Welsh Rarebit' was Gladys Morgan, a four foot ten inches 'force of nature', who featured every week in comic conversations with the programme's smooth, charming, and mild-mannered announcer, Alun Williams. Gladys told anecdotes rather than jokes, all related in a strong Swansea accent and punctuated at times by her outrageous ear-splitting, cackling laugh. Even when we were all growing up in the sixties, one could hear a 'Gladys' in any cafe or any corner of Swansea Market.

Light Programme on Thursday, 11th May

The programme, which was broadcast nationally on Thursday, 11th May, 1950 from 9.00 p.m. to 10 p.m on the Light Programme, included the following cast:
Tano Ferendinos, Des Williams, Albert and Les Ward, Harry Secombe, Ann Walters, Frank James, Frank Davison, The Girls in Harmony,
The Swansea Imperial Singers,
'The Adventures of Tommy Troubles' script by E. Eynon Evans)
The Welsh Variety Orchestra (leader, Morgan Lloyd) produced by Mai Jones.

The role of Announcer in this particular episode was taken by Frank James. Olive was never able to meet her comic heroine in person. However, an autographed photo of Harry Secombe remained in pride of place on top of the Rees living-room radiogram for many years.

Harry has always been to the Rees family, Swansea's most famous son.

'Welsh Rarebit' was recorded at Cardiff's Corey Hall which, according to Harry, was acoustically excellent, if lacking in other vital facilities such as toilets! Oh! The romance of show business!

'The Western Mail' was quick to take notice of the Imperials' presence on the programme, with a welcome if rather inaccurate piece of praise,
'Congratulations to that genial musician, Mr. Jack Newbury and his Swansea Imperial Singers on their first all-Britain broadcast on 'Welsh Rarebit'. They have done a lot of tuneful broadcasting in the Welsh programmes for years.'

The choir had first been invited to participate in an episode of 'Welsh Rarebit' broadcast in April 1947 on the Welsh Home Service, and they had already made their debut on British national radio earlier in the Spring.

The Imperials' hectic schedule continued through the summer of 1950 with another recording of an episode of 'Welsh Rarebit' on Thursday, 15th June.

Once again the programme was broadcast at its regular time of 9.00p.m.

'Welsh Rarebit' on Thursday, 15th June

This time the star billing read as follows:
Zoe Creswell, Des Williams, Ossie Morris, Ann Walters, Frank James, Frank Davison,
The Girls in Harmony,
The Swansea Imperials Singers – conductor Jack Newbury,
The Adventures of Tommy Troubles' – script by E. Eynon Evans
The Welsh Variety Orchestra (leader Morgan Lloyd) produced by Mai Jones.

Three weeks later the choir were rewarded with their very own 30 minute programme for the Welsh Home Service, recorded in Swansea. There is no description of, or title for this programme but we can probably guess from the choir's records what they would have sung. Similar programmes in the choir's name were broadcast in 1951, not just across Wales but the other Celtic nations of the Union, including one in which the choir's records were played. Temporarily, it seems in 1951 the choir stood back from the limelight. Geoff believes he may have been the cause of this as he was born in May of that year, and Olive would have had to withdraw from her choir commitments for a while.

In the late Spring of 1952 the BBC finally fulfilled its promise to restore their burned out studios in Alexandra Road. Following on immediately after the required speeches by civic dignitaries and representatives of the BBC 'Sut Hwyl' became the first programme to be broadcast from the 'ultra modern studio 1' which provided room, not only for the usual company of players and instrumentalists, but also for a choir and orchestra - .... 'The Swansea Imperial Singers' and the BBC Welsh Orchestra, conducted by Rae Jenkins!

The massive Port Talbot Steel Works opened its gates

1951

An early press photograph of the Abbey Steel Works at Port Talbot, Wales

Abbey Steel Works at Port Talbot, Wales, UK. It was opened in 1951 and was fully operational by 1953.

There may have been other high profile opportunities that followed but on 'The Radio Times' site, after this succession of programmes, the choir seems to disappear from the limelight until the beginning of 1953.

There were important changes and opportunities arising in the lives of the men of the choir, as ICI began to open new factories through the 1950s, the massive Port Talbot Steel Works opened its gates, and as some choir members began to find new homes. Ivor Rees helped to install some of the old Landore rolling stock in the new metal manufacturing plants in Waunarlwydd. The day to day easy contact between core members of the choir may have begun to fracture.

Stave 11

'Waxing lyrical'

1950

© Oleksiy Mark Shutterstock

In a programme aired on the Home Service, conductor Jack Newbury discussed the gramophone records which the choir had made on the Decca label, in January 1950.

This was followed up on Wednesday 13th May, on the Home Service, when the records were played on air. Once again, how wonderful it would be to be able to hear Jack's authoritative voice and the choir singing through their core repertoire, ... but sadly, no recording of either of these programmes still exists.

There are nine songs on the four records. 'Laudamus' (Bryn Calfaria) is a famous Welsh hymn by William Owen (1813 – 43). He is said to have composed the song on a piece of slate as he walked to work at a quarry in Gwynedd, North Wales. The musical arrangement is by Dr. Daniel Protheroe (1866 – 1934),

MADE IN ENGLAND

DECCA

THE SUPREME RECORD

THE DECCA RECD RECORD CO LTD

I P

DAFYDD Y GARREG WEN

(D. Protheroe)

THE SWANSEA IMPERIAL SINGERS

Conductor : JACK NEWBURY

Sung in Welsh

DR.14480
A

CHAPPELL & CO LD
LONDON

F.9419

who was a celebrated Welsh composer and conductor born near Ystradgynlais at the top of the Swansea Valley where there is a memorial dedicated to him. Something of a child prodigy, Dr. Protheroe left Wales for the United States at the age of 19 and became an important musical celebrity in Chicago. The Welsh Imperials heard his famous choir in concert when they visited 'The Windy City' in December 1931, and would probably have met the great man. Dan Protheroe regularly returned to his homeland and officiated at National Eisteddfods including Swansea's in 1926. His influence on traditional Welsh music can be seen and heard here on a number of the Imperials' tracks.

'O Mor Ber', or 'In the Sweet bye and bye' is another Protheroe setting of a Welsh hymn which features a fine solo performance by baritone and choir Secretary, Alwyn Edwards.

Dafydd y Garreg Wen was **Stanley Unwin's** choice for Desert Island Discs in 1962.

Mario Lanza

The records feature several other familiar beautiful, haunting melodies such as **'Llwyn Onn' ('The Ash Grove')**, a traditional song of lost love, and **'Ar Hyd Y Nos' ('All Through the Night')** first notated in 1784. The version used by the Imperials was arranged by Roland Rogers and uses lyrics by the Welsh poet, John Ceiriog Hughes.

'Dacw Nghariddi (i lawr yn y berllan)' or **'There is my sweetheart down in the orchard'** also portrays the heartache and a yearning for love and has become a very popular recording choice for modern Welsh performers, both male and female.

The song that Geoff recalls his father singing most at home, "his tenor voice soaring above and about me," however, was **'Bendithia'r Ty'**, which is known more famously as **'Bless This House'**, and was a standard performance piece for tenors such as Mario Lanza and Harry Secombe at this time. This powerful melody was composed by the Australian Mary Hannah (May) Brahe (1884 – 1956) and published in 1927 with words by her English-born friend Helen Taylor. The Imperials give the song a resounding, emotional performance that remains with the listener for a long while afterwards.

The beautiful records could be purchased from Snell's Music Shop on the corner of the Arcade and High Street, just along from High Street Railway Station. One Neath shop's newspaper advert in the Spring of 1950 listed together recordings by **Tito Gobbi, Gigli, Donald Peers, The Swansea Imperials and Perry Como. Such elevated company indeed!**

All the choir members received copies of the discs **which were made from wax and needed to be carefully handled** so that they did not get scratched.

'My parents' records lay on top of a wardrobe to be played occasionally on my brother's cream and red, Dansette record-player, but they disappeared after my mother passed away in 1989.'
Geoff Rees

However, we can still enjoy the beauty of the choir's voices thanks to John Hayward's father, Ern, who relished his time in the choir and treated his copies of the records like treasure.

'My father used to play the records through a 1940s Ambassador radiogram which had a lovely warm sound. He had an evening of playing them every two to three months. The highlight for me was the choir's comic encore item of **'Dr. Foster'**, a musical arrangement by Irish composer, Herbert Hughes of a nursery rhyme, sung with the dignity and intricate harmonies of a Handel chorus – especially the very low bass parts at the end. As a child, I could never really understand why grown men were singing a children's song. Now I understand, and I will be playing Dr. Foster to my grandchildren.'

'Doctor Foster went to Gloucester in a shower of rain,
He stepped in a puddle,
Right up to his middle,
And never went there again ...'

John carefully preserved his father's collection and, thanks to him, it has been possible to 'burn' CDs of the records so that each of us involved in this project has been able to enjoy them. For our little collection of contributors, this has been a very emotional experience.

Professor Stanley Unwin

© Maloney/ANL/Shutterstock

Terry Scott and Stanley Unwin, October 1973.

At Christmastime 1956, in a celebratory programme, entitled **'Lleisiau Meibion'** and intended to display the tremendous talent of male-voice singing in the Swansea area in the post-war era, the records of 'The Swansea Imperials', Morriston Orpheus and Manselton Male-Voice were featured.

The choir's recordings had many admirers, one of whom was actor, comedian and celebrity 'Professor' Stanley Unwin who chose **'Dafydd Y Garreg Wen'** by the Swansea Imperials as one of his **'Desert Island Discs'** when he was the guest of Roy Plomley's iconic programme on Monday 10th September, 1962.

Stanley was brought up in a National Children's home - first in Congleton, Cheshire, and then educated at the Henry Gibb Nautical School in Penarth (now Headlands School). Each Sunday the boys would march to and from Trinity Methodist Church in Penarth and so Stanley may have remembered some of the Welsh Hymns and music sung there.

He also worked as an Outside Broadcast Engineer for the BBC as part of the War Correspondent Unit, covering historic events such as the D-Day Landings and

The Peace Conference in 1946, before breaking into 'show business', and travelling the UK with various producers and presenters such as Godfrey Bazeley, Wynford Vaughan-Thomas, Richard Dimbleby and many more. He recorded a variety of programmes including 'Farm Visit' and 'Down Your Way' as well as individual artists such as Harry Secombe and Pablo Casals. Stanley's daughter, Lois thinks that it is likely that her father made recordings of the Swansea Imperials at that time. 'If he did, then he certainly would have remembered and felt nostalgic about it as he was very fond of that style of music.'

Stanley may have recorded the choir when they were at the peak of their powers in the late 1940s – early 1950s, during one of his frequent visits to Wales. This North Walian song, like several others on the choir's records, was a staple element of the Welsh and Swansea Imperials' concert programmes. It is said to have been composed by David Owen (1712 – 41), a harpist and composer from Porthmadog. He was known as **'Dafydd Y Garreg Wen' or 'David of the White Rock',** after the farm where he lived. The legend states that as he lay on his deathbed, Dafydd called for his harp and composed this deeply moving melody.

Alas, once again, no audio recording remains of Stanley Unwin's 'Desert Island' choices which is a great pity. He was very entertaining in interviews and famous for the use of his comic, made-up language which some called 'Unwinese', but which he referred to as 'Double Talk'.

For an example of it, Stanley was known to have referred to Beethoven as 'Beethovey' and Mozart as 'Mozarkers'! One wonders what he would have made of the Welsh language title of this famous song! In reality, he loved music and, apart from the Imperials, his 'Desert Island' favourites included classical works by Beethoven, Franck, Johann Sebastian Bach, and Liszt and more popular vocals by Peter Dawson and the truly great Ella Fitzgerald.

Recently, a transcript of the programme, courtesy of the BBC, has become available and it is clear from it that Stanley applied much thought to his choice of music. 'Well at first I made a list of about 20 or 30 or so and chose a few, and then I put that on one side, and made another selection, and in the result it became more or less a compromise between one's favourites and the number of memories that could be conjured up ... and the actual sheer enjoyment of the music for its own sake, composer, executor and so on.'

'Is Music important to you?'
'In the dull days of the Slump and in the early 30s and not able to enjoy oneself a great deal in one's spare time, I found an escape to music being a wonderful thing to help me carry on.'

His eighth and last choice of piano music by Liszt is lovingly dedicated to his two talented daughters. In all the articles we have read about Stanley, he is always referred to as a fine, kind-hearted and modest man, and the authors of this book are very proud that someone so good-natured and musically astute should have selected a work by 'The Swansea Imperials' for his special list.

To listen to the records by the Swansea Imperials mentioned in this chapter, access their YouTube channel, youtube.com/@swanseaimperialsingers

Stave 12

Swan song

Stan Stennett

Stan Stennett, who starred in the BBC light programme Welsh Rarebit, January 1953.

At some point in the mid-1950s, the Swansea Imperials seem to have disbanded. Jack, now over 50, and with a young family, may have begun to tire of his role as muse, organiser and musical director of the choir, a role that he had fulfilled admirably for nearly 20 years. Radio was losing ground to television. A recent Radio 4 programme claimed that 1953 was the year in which more people admitted to watching TV than to listening to the wireless.

Some of the Wales-inspired radio programmes like 'Welsh Rarebit' had run their course.

There were other superb choirs in which Jack and the others could participate. He was a member of the all-conquering Morriston Orpheus choir who won four consecutive Eisteddfod first prizes from 1946 to 1949, and his wife Carrie was a member of the Morriston Ladies Choir.

'I met Jack only once when I was about six years old and when my father, Ivor, and I called at his house in Bath Road, Morriston while out on one of our Sunday morning walks, which usually ended up in the Italian ice-cream shop on Brynhyfryd Square. I was rather shy when I was small, but I sensed that Jack and Carrie were lovely people who were very fond of my father.

They were very kind and welcoming to me and gave me two toy corgi cars, a blue Riley Pathfinder, and a cream Austin Cambridge which belonged to their son, Phil, who is four years older than me. In 2019 I met Phil for the first time, and, some 60 years later, I was able to solve the riddle of his missing cars and to reassure him that they had always been looked after and passed on intact to the next generation!" **Geoff Rees**

Frank Newbury joined another choir in the early 1950s and it was after a performance at one of its concerts that he met Catherine Lily Rees. They wed in August 1952. Throughout his life, singing continued to be very important to Frank. Parishioners of Clyne Chapel still recall his wonderful baritone voice harmonising to the hymns.

His last performance was a sterling rendering of the 'Bold Gendarmes' as a duet with his brother-in-law, Jim Hurford, another great singer, in the Church Hall at Holy Cross when Frank was into his eighties. When doing jobs around the house or in the garden or driving, he would often sing. His repertoire was not composed solely of classical or religious songs, but also more modern pieces, always delivered with a strong resonant voice. Frank had a passion for words and could recall exactly poems that he had memorised at school. His favourite was **'The Daffodils' by William Wordsworth.** The lines of its last verse seem so appropriate in the context of this book of fond memories,

'For oft when on my couch I lie
In vacant or in pensive mood,
They flash upon that inward eye
Which is the bliss of solitude;
And then my heart with pleasure fills,
And dances with the daffodils.'

In February, 1953, Ivor, Olive and their two sons moved out of the centre of Swansea and into a new council house in Ewenny Place, Clase, an estate poised on the hilly fringes of the town. There continued to be a steady stream of visitors who came to their house to rehearse with the help of Olive's accompanist skills.

'Most of them were pretty, young sopranos who wanted to practise light operatic numbers, or songs like 'So in Love' from the musical 'Kiss Me Kate' for their roles in amateur productions or for their personal solo repertoire. We had an old, much-cherished, black upright piano in our front room with 'Crane & Sons of London' emblazoned just above the lid over the keys. I was fascinated by the gold lettering and the strange shaped ampersand which lay just on my eye-line and how my mother's hands danced elegantly across the keys."

Geoff Rees

In the 1960s, Olive helped out playing the piano for women's keep-fit classes, such as the one held in Mynyddbach School, but at the weekends she toured the South Wales clubs with a small concert party, opening a new exciting area of adventure in her life. Typically, she used very little of her fees on herself and would send Geoff weekly 'pocket-money' when he was at University to 'treat' himself.

*'I vividly remember my father standing and singing at my mother's side when I was young, and I was sometimes encouraged to learn a song or duet myself that I could perform to visitors, standing on the piano stool. At Christmas, **'Little Donkey'** was my pièce de résistance, I recall.*

However, after about 1960, when he turned fifty, I do not recall Dad singing at all in the house. Unlike many of the other Imperials, he was not a member of a chapel where he may have continued to perform with others. What does fix itself in my memory is how hard he was working at the new I.M.I Titanium Plant – seven days-a-week – and how tired he always was when he came home from the factory of an evening. After tea he would nearly always have a sleep for an hour in his arm-chair with his feet supported by an old wooden upright chair and with our beautiful, black and white cat contentedly stretched out along the length of his legs.

'The Bold Gendarmes!' at the Landore Long Service Awards Presentation

1961

Photo courtesy of ICI magazines

To confound these memories, I recently found a photo of **my father (1)** and **Jack Newbury (2)** and **Cecil Lewis (3)** in an October 1961 copy of the Yorkshire Imperial Magazine, where they are offering a full-blooded rendition of **'The Bold Gendarmes!' at the Landore Long Service Awards Presentation,** held earlier in that year in the Swansea Guildhall on Friday 26th May.

Despite the caption's reference to the 'Choir', I believe this was an impromptu piece of community singing to enhance the evening, rather than the reforming of the Imperials 'for one night only', ... but for Phil Newbury and me it is a heart-warming picture, showing just how much our fathers continued to love singing and performing."

Geoff Rees

Ivor often told Geoff things about his youth but virtually nothing about the choir. "Perhaps he thought my older brother and I would not be interested. While he loved radio classics such as 'A Hundred Best Tunes', and 'Sing Something Simple' with the Adams Singers, we wanted 'Pick of the Pops' and Radio Luxembourg. My brother's idols were Bill Haley, Elvis and Buddy Holly – mine were 'The Beatles', Gerry and the Pacemakers' and 'The Searchers'. Perhaps there has never been such a generational shift in musical tastes as there was in the 1950s and early 1960s. It was an era when sales of guitars went through the roof !

My father was a very unassuming, and modest man, a very good man with high expectations of behaviour. I owe him so much. Without the example of his standards and of his work ethic, I would never have achieved what I have in my life. My mother was simply the kindest person I have ever known. She lived on after my father's passing in 1976 to love and treasure her sons and grandchildren in her later years." **Geoff Rees**

Tal Griffiths continued with his other musical connections and he had many different interests too.

Tal was a keen gardener and belonged to Morriston Horticultural Society. He was also an important official of a trade union and would travel to Bristol for monthly meetings. Like many of the men in the choir he was very skilful practically. His grand-daughter, Andrea recalls that Tal made all the furniture for her bedroom – a fitted wardrobe and drawers, a desk and even a dressing table, as well as a fort, a doll's cot and various other wooden items for any relative or friend who asked. Andrea remembers Tal as 'an amazing story-teller, from his mouth as opposed to reading from books'.

Ern played bowls throughout the summer and loved gardening and walking. Amusingly, John relates that Ern *'may have spent 48 years painting cars but he never learned to drive one!'*

Ern Hayward, also continued in other musical societies. He was for many years a member of the Argyle Chapel Choir in St. Helen's Road. The conductor, the Reverend D. Reginald Thomas, was highly skilled in musical production and the choir would attempt very ambitious works such as 'The Messiah'. When Reverend Thomas left Argyle in 1955, the choir disintegrated and Ern joined the Brunswick Chapel Choir while also performing with an informal group of singers who held rehearsals at the home of leader Percy Davies. This group performed at Christmas occasions and at other events in the year. Poignantly, when a choir member was ill, the others would gather outside his home to sing and comfort those within.

Coda by Geoff Rees

For many years I never considered contributing
to a book about 'The Swansea Imperials'. I did not
know enough, I did not know of the success that they
achieved, and I wondered if there was anyone else
who cared about the choir....... and then my son, David,
found John Hayward's Facebook page about his father,
Ernest, which in itself is a wonderful memorial to
the Imperials.

A request from John and myself for more people to
come forward, kindly hosted by the Evening Post's
Robert Lloyd, aroused the interest of two more key
contributors, Jack's son, Phil and Tal's granddaughter,
Andrea who loved and respected their ancestors.
More recently Brinley Hurford and Colin Williams
kindly contributed affectionate memories of their
uncles, Frank Newbury and Ken Williams.

Singing is a wonderful thing. It has the power to lift
one's heart and soul. I think we were all so lucky to
live in homes full of melodies which constantly swirled
around us as we were growing up.

The 'Imperials' lived through difficult times but
singing and performing was their joyful medicine and
their balm, and they have endowed each of us with a
life-long love of song.

This was their special gift to us. This little book is our gift and memorial to them.

The Singers on one of their family excursions in the 1950s

'Thank you for the music'

Acknowledgements

Creating 'The Love of Song' in a time of Covid

The authors began discussions for this little book in July 2019. However, the actual writing began in February 2020 just days before the first Covid lockdown.

This made further research extremely difficult. Letters and emails went unanswered, and public buildings were closed. However, as you will read below, there were those who responded and helped us gather vital information throughout this extraordinary time.

The authors would like to acknowledge and thank the following sources and contributors:

Gwasg Carreg Gwalch, the Publishers of Alun Trevor's brilliant book 'The Welsh Imperial Singers';

'Down the Memory Lanes of MY HAFOD' by J. Ramsey Kilpatrick with Felicity Kilpatrick;

Swansea Library Staff, for their advice and fantastic support in accessing 'The South Wales Evening Post' and 'Herald of Wales' Archives;

West Glamorgan Archives and Dr. David Morris for help in selecting and providing historic photos of Swansea;

Swansea Museum and Emma Williams for providing the photo of the Landore Works complex;

The performance diary of Ivor Owen, courtesy of West Glamorgan Archives;

'Undefeated – The Triumphs and Tragedies of Rocky Marciano' by Mike Stanton;

The Autobiographies of Harry Secombe;

The BBC - 'Funny Nation' by Elis James;

The BBC online 'Genome Project' which contains all the back numbers of 'The Radio Times';

'British Newspapers Online' and Hilary Williams of the Brecon Family History Society for making me aware of this terrific resource;

The Family of Stanley Unwin, in particular Lois, Stanley's daughter, who kindly responded to a letter posted to her parish church during the earliest and most alarming period of the pandemic, and provided so much information about her father;

Robert Lloyd of 'The South Wales Evening Post' for his advice, and for publishing the article about the Singers in April 2019 which brought the authors together, and the newspaper for granting permission to print two pictures and a section of an article;

'The Western Mail' for publishing a letter which resulted in further responses from relatives of the choir.

'Swansea City F.C.' – by John Burgum and **'Swansea Town Football Club** 1912 – 1964' compiled by Richard Shepherd;

'Morriston Hospital: The Early Years' – by Dewi Glannant Williams;

'Swansea at War' by Sally Bowler;

The Family Photograph, Letter and Record Collections of Geoff Rees, John Hayward, Phil Newbury and Colin Williams;

Samantha Blake at BBC 'Heritage' and Paula McGinley of 'Desert Island Discs'. The transcripts of programmes in which the Singers performed told us many important things about the choir of which we had been unaware previously;

Bill Sterio, Peter Barker and Margaret Fox, Leighton Radford, Leah Fenlon and Keith Plummer ... close friends of the authors who read the three drafts of this book and offered advice;

Gareth Watkins, for his invaluable help in proof-reading the three drafts;

Ann Grey for help with Frank's story;

Dylan Thomas – 'Return Journey' and 'Extraordinary Little Cough';

The lectures of J. R. Alban (hosted by West Glamorgan Archives) and his masterly work 'The Three Night's Blitz';

'Operation Wasservogel' – by R.T. Pearce for its detailed and moving account of the last bombing raid on Swansea in 1943;

ICI Magazines;

The Swansea Wartime Diary of Laurie Latchford;

The Oral Recordings of Cecil Lewis (courtesy of West Glamorgan Archives);

'Do You Hear the People Sing?' Gareth Williams (published by Gomer);

Diana Edwards of Diana Edwards Design and Gareth Acreman of Gomer Press for their invaluable assistance in the design and print of this book;

Elaine Kidwell and Geoff Jones who gave fascinating interviews to the children at Pentrehafod School for their project on the Americans in Swansea – part of a wider plan of research promoted by Donald Anderson M.P. on behalf of the American Embassy in London in the year 2000;

Stephen Jones for allowing us to publish a small section of his father's memoirs.

Swansea Imperials 'YouTube' channel created by John Hayward youtube.com/@swanseaimperialsingers

Geoff's cousin-in-law, Jean Pratchett, for her family research skills;

Geoff's cousin David Burn for his knowledge of Rees family history;

Barbara Jones for help with her father Ern's story;

David Rees, and Chris Rees whose affection for their grandmother led to the initial meeting of the co-authors of this book, and who helped Geoff to overcome his fear of technology;

Our wives Fran, Janet and Helen, for their patience and assistance during the research and writing of this book and for being our adored and constant inspiration;

And finally … **the doctors, nurses, community nurses, radiologists and vaccinators who helped to keep ourselves, our families and our friends safe over the past three years;**
GR/JH/PH

'I should like to bury something precious in every place where I've been happy and then, when I was old …, I could come back and dig it up and remember.'

(from 'Brideshead Revisited' by Evelyn Waugh)

Our book focuses on a small number of participants in The Swansea Imperials. The authors are aware that many others played leading parts in the success of the choir such as **Walter James, Edgar Richards**, and **Horace Evans** but information about them was not forthcoming at the time of publication.

However, during the writing of this book, a little additional biographical information has arisen about some members of the choir. **George Owen** and **Ben Davies** were both ICI men, experienced choral singers and stalwart, long-serving members of the Imperial Singers, and appear in nearly all the choir's photos.

Joe Dennis, a fine bass/baritone, and a stalwart of the choir in the Post-War years, lived in Pantycelyn Road, Townhill – an avenue which offers the finest panoramic views of Swansea. Joe's son, **Haydn Dennis** was for some years Minister of York Place Baptist Church.

Emlyn Phillips was another 'Imperial' and a member of Caersalem Baptist Chapel, Tirdeinaw. Emlyn's sister, **Kate** was also a fine singer and a member of Dinas Noddfa Baptist Church where she frequently gave solos during chapel services. 'In the past, the locality bounded by Brynhyfryd, Mynyddbach and Morriston produced many quality singers.'(Colin Williams)

Cecil Lewis was a very good friend of both **Ivor Rees** and **Jack Newbury**. He worked at ICI Landore before WW2, rising from a messenger boy to become foreman over a large area of the works. He organised many entertaining events for the workers and had wide experience of singing in Swansea with various choirs. Two of the more extraordinary places in which he sang as a young man were the Ben Evans Department Store at one of the many Sunday evening services held there, and the Swansea Workhouse !

Alwyn Edwards was also a work colleague of some of the choir members. He was the redoubtable secretary of The Swansea Imperials during their halcyon days in the late 40s, early 50s, and was the fine soloist on one of the choir's records.

Tommy Horn, also possessed of a fine voice, became the choir's librarian, busily ordering and organising music during the Imperials' hectic post-war schedule.

The authors would love to hear from anyone with further information about any of the Imperials.

Geoff

John

Phil

Geoff Rees

Was educated at Kent University and St. Luke's College, Exeter in the early 1970s. However, he reserves his greatest gratitude for his teachers at Penlan Comprehensive School, Swansea – 'Mr Robins, Mr Jones, Mr Benjamin and Mr Day – who inspired my love of English Literature, the Theatre and History.'

Although 'For the Love of Song' Is Geoff's first 'named' association with a widely-published work, he has been a writer all his life. In a long and successful teaching career in London and Swansea, he wrote numerous stories, and created a host of writing models for school, while adapting many difficult works of literature to make them more accessible to his pupils.

Since his retirement in 2011, Geoff has participated in several local history projects, and collaborated with relatives from around the UK in extensive family research.

Born in the centre of Swansea, in a flat equidistantly situated between St. Helen's Cricket and Rugby Ground and the Vetch Field, it was perhaps predictable that his other life-long passions have been cricket and football. Geoff is well-known in local cricketing circles as a player, youth coach and administrator, and has been supporting Swansea Town and City since 1958 ... 'through thick and thin'.

Geoff has been married to Fran, a singer and musician herself, for 49 years. 'Imagine my parents' delight when they discovered that Fran possessed a beautiful voice.' They have two sons and four grandchildren.

'I was brought up in a small close-knit and loving family, and these days, my family and friends mean everything to me.'

Esmond Rees

Our book would be incomplete without a tribute to Geoff's older brother, Esmond, who preserved and annotated their parents' photos after the death of their mother, Olive in 1989

He was bright academically, but preferred to leave school at sixteen and take the practical route into a career in industry. Starting out as an apprentice toolmaker with ICI, Es worked all over South Wales including in a works making parts for Concorde. However, in 1977 he became Quality Control Manager at Avon Inflatables in Dafen and settled back in Swansea. He was held in high regard by shop-floor staff and Management alike at the Llanelli life-boat plant.

'Sadly, Es, my dear, talented and handsome brother passed away in November 2001 at the age of just 61.

Geoff writes, despite an age difference of more than ten years, we became best friends in adult life. Es was always, my 'big brother'. As a boy, I read all his twenty 'William' books, because he had read them; as a teenager, I wore some of his hand-me-downs because he had worn them with style, and as a hopeless, ham-fisted academic in later life, I tried to listen intently when he explained some complicated mechanical process, for Es could build, or repair anything. We never panicked if something or some gadget went wrong, for we knew Es could and would fix it.

After the passing of my father, Es lovingly looked after our mother, creating her own personal room in his family house, where she lived in peace and security for the last ten years of her life

Our parents never boasted to us about their musical achievements. Life and fashions changed so much in the 1950s and 1960s that perhaps they felt that we wouldn't be interested,

Olive Rees and her son Esmond, Autumn 1940.

'but I'm sure today that they and my 'big brother' would more than approve of this humble little book about the much-loved Swansea Imperial Singers..'

John Hayward

Was born in Swansea and brought up just across the street from Victoria park. As a child, if he wasn't in the park, he was playing on Swansea beach with his friends! It was an idyllic setting in which to grow up.

After attending Brynmill and Bishop Gore Schools, John left Swansea to study at Queen Mary College London, where he graduated with bachelors and doctorate degrees in astrophysics. After a period of research in astronomy, he pursued a career as a mathematics lecturer in Scotland and latterly at the University of South Wales. He has a number of publications in the field of mathematical modelling and remains research-active in retirement.

John is married to Helen, whom he met as a student in London. After retirement, they moved back to Scotland, where they pursue their love of gardening and the great outdoors. They have two children and four grandchildren who fill their lives with much joy.

John has a keen interest in family history, tracing some lines back to antiquity and finding relatives across the world.

'It has been a joy to apply these family history skills to the Swansea Imperial Singers, the choir my father always talked about and whose records he treasured so much.'

John did not inherit his father's gift of singing. Instead, he expressed his love of music through the electric guitar, which he has played in various church music groups.

'How I loved the sands in Swansea! It was heaven.'

Phil Newbury

Is the son of Jack, the Swansea Imperials' charismatic leader, conductor, and inspiration. Phil was born on 9th January, 1947, during one of the worst winters on record in South Wales.

His mother Carrie was being cared for in the specialist maternity hospital at Stouthall, near the village of Reynoldston in the heart of rural Gower. 'This created a very taxing visiting experience for my father who was working at ICI in Landore and living in Morriston right over the other side of Swansea.' However, Jack coped with this situation with typical energy, devotion and commitment. 'The service buses would only take him so far, especially after a fall of snow, but he would happily tackle on foot the remaining ten miles or so across the Gower countryside to reach the isolated unit.'

Carrie and her new-born son were eventually allowed home to their house in Bath Road, Morriston which overlooked the heavily industrialised Lower Swansea Valley.

After negotiating the dreaded 'eleven-plus' exams, Phil was educated at Dynevor Grammar School in Swansea town centre.

'I would catch the number 77 red double-decker bus every morning, stepping off in Oxford Street, and visit the famous market for a copy of 'The New Musical Express'. My musical tastes were very different to those of my parents at that time.

Influenced by his Uncle Frank Newbury's success, Phil followed him into a career with the Post Office, rising gradually to senior managerial posts. Promotion meant moving to Newport where he now lives with his wife Janet, who has also contributed substantially to the completion of this book.

'Leaving Swansea was really hard. Swansea was my enchanted town with its dramatic hills and lovely beaches when I was growing up. The town centre was very busy with a wide range of shops and cinemas like The Plaza, The Albert Hall, The Castle and The Carlton, showing all manner of films'

'One of my happiest memories is of the walk from Mumbles round to the beautiful Langland Bay. Some relatives had a beach hut there, which, incredibly, they used to dismantle every late Autumn and rebuild the following Spring. I spent many happy hours there.'

'It's been a wonderful experience researching the lives and times of our parents, and what we have learnt about their friendships has brought the three of us very close together. When I think back ... we might never have met but for an article which Geoff and John placed with Robert Lloyd at 'The Evening Post' in April 2019.

My nephew read it and immediately contacted me. And the rest as they say 'is history'. John had already created a Facebook page for the choir while Geoff had inherited lots of photos of the Imperials. The one name that Geoff had heard his parents constantly use when he was a young boy was that of my father, 'Jack Newbury'.

'We've all learned a new perspective, a new overview of our parents' achievements, and listening to their recordings has become a very emotional experience for all three of us.'

'Unlocking the past' by Geoff Rees

'The past is a foreign country. They do things differently there.' This much quoted opening line of L.P. Hartley's novel, 'The Go-Between', has real resonance for the authors of this book, because although extensive research has gone into making our story as accurate as we can, at its heart, **'For The Love of Song'** is a collection of memories of our parents and we were very young when **The Swansea Imperial Singers were in their hey-day.** During the writing of this book, a curious thing happened. We all became those small persons again, desperately trying to recall the words, music and events that were swirling over and around us. Some recollections were clearer than others. Where we couldn't verify a memory we had to leave it out.

At the beginning of 2019, my son David made a glorious discovery – a lovingly designed Facebook page devoted to Ernest Hayward's war diary and created by his son John Hayward, which featured pictures of the Imperial Singers and their records. Whereas my parents' recordings have been lost over time, John's father had preserved his copies of the records and played them regularly, recalling so many fond memories of his time with the choir. Ernest and my father Ivor had both sung with the Swansea and District Royal Male Voice Choir and I had photos too of this prestigious ensemble. After an exchange of memories and photos, John and I submitted an article to 'The South Wales Evening Post' stating that we were researching the Swansea Imperials and inviting others who had information to contact us.

At the same time we were aware of an earlier choir which had used the name Imperial – The Welsh Imperial Singers. Could there be a connection between the two? On the same day that the article appeared in the paper we had two wonderful responses. The first by Andrea Davies concerned her grandfather, Tal Griffiths, for whom she had very affectionate memories. Tal was an original founder and influential member of the choir who sang with the Imperials throughout their existence. The second email came from our co-author, Phil Newbury, son of Jack Newbury, the hugely talented singer, conductor and driving force of the choir. I met Phil almost the next day outside the Liberty Stadium before a Swans match. Phil lives in Newport but had been alerted to the article by his relative, Brinley Hurford, who also later contributed vivid memories of his uncle, Frank Newbury. From that day, in April 2019, John and I knew we would be able to compose a book worthy of the choir's history.

Three months later in July, John, and Phil visited my house and we began to plan a way forward. From my brother I had inherited a cache of photos of choirs in which our father had participated, but my memories only extended back to my own childhood. John and Phil's knowledge, however, could take us back much further, beyond World War II and even into the 1920s. Phil revealed that his father had indeed sung with the Welsh Imperials and had toured Canada and America on four occasions with them in the 1920s and 1930s. He had knowledge of these tours, a postcard from Chicago, dated from 1938, which was very informative and an article written by his uncle about Jack from the 1980s. Clearly, 'The Welsh Imperials' had to be our starting point.

Soon after this meeting the serious work of detailed research began. At this stage, two inspirational, carefully researched and beautifully written works of family history by Alun Trevor and Felicity Kilpatrick acted as models for our project. By January 2020 the actual drafting of our book had begun.

Alas, little did we know what lay just around the corner! On March 23rd, the United Kingdom went into lockdown to protect the nation from Covid, and all public buildings, including libraries, archives, studios and chapels were closed to access. In the next few months, many letters and emails were sent out, but most of them simply fell on the floors of empty offices or remained unnoticed on the laptops at vacant desks. There were so many disappointments.

However, when responses came they lit up what was otherwise a dark time for us all. First, I had a very thoughtful phone call from the offices of IMI Waunarlwydd, where my father, Ivor Rees, had spent his final working years. Then I received a wonderful email from Lois Johnston, the daughter of Stanley Unwin, giving us permission to include her father's part in the Imperials' story. Finally, there was a brilliant reply from the offices of 'Desert Island Discs' at BBC's Broadcasting House. There would not be any audio tapes of programmes that the choir made still in existence, 'but' the letter went on, 'there is still hope' – I will always remember those words! **Thank heavens for the BBC!**

The second half of the letter informed me that transcripts of their programmes might still be accessed at the BBC's archive heritage site in Reading. An enquiry met with an instant and uplifting answer. **There were transcripts of several of the choir's most high-profile programmes**. These gave us much new information and enabled us to discover how the choir originated, and developed. The transcripts also revealed to us a previously unknown fact – that the Swansea Imperials had raised 'thousands of pounds' for local charities, in particular Singleton Hospital and St. John's Ambulance.

Further discoveries were made once the lock-down was eased. Swansea Library and Archives, with their terrifically helpful and knowledgeable staff, had opened their doors again. There is much news coverage which can be gleaned online, but for local Swansea history, **there is no substitute for back-numbers of 'The South Wales Evening Post' and 'Herald of Wales'. Newspapers** in every year from 1938 to 1956 were scrutinised, and there, amongst other fascinating stories of the time, lay previews and reviews of their concerts and performances, photographs of the Imperials, and the names of nearly all of the singers!

The choir began as an octet but grew into a larger ensemble of sixteen to seventeen singers after the War. Membership of the choir changed a little from time to time, but the core of the choir remained the same. We have only included detailed information about individuals where relatives like Colin Williams have contacted us, or where special information was already in the public domain. Cecil Lewis, for instance, recorded his time working in the Hafod-Morfa Copperworks for the Archives, and Hugh Cann's record of honourable public service was reported in detail in 'The Evening Post', 'Western Mail' and elsewhere. However, we feel that our research into the performances, the records, the many photos and the names of the choir will have brought back all the choristers to public notice and to a generation who knew nothing about these talented singers and musicians. If this book persuades just a few readers to research family ancestors, to simply speak to their mothers, fathers or elderly relatives about their lives and achievements, our efforts will have been worthwhile.

By December 2021, our exploratory first draft had more than tripled in size. The document was patiently and professionally copied for us by Raul Rucarean at his photography business in St. Helen's Road Swansea. This enabled us to post the draft to our 'family' of proof-readers for criticism. Raul also recommended Gomer for the publication of our book. The choir had been formed in Swansea, had often sung in Welsh and we felt it fitting that any book about them should be printed in Wales.

I began by describing **'For the Love of Song' as 'a book of memories' ... of our parents, grandparents, their friends, their times and of the town which they loved.** There is one special memory which I return to time and again and has remained with me throughout our writing of this book. I was only about 6 years old at the time. ICI was a very generous and considerate employer. Jack, Tal and my father, Ivor all felt happy there and secure in their jobs. ICI was where their working friendships began and where the original Imperial Octet came into being. Every Christmas the works threw a party for the children of its employees which both my brother and I attended. The **parties usually consisted of a short movie, starring Charlie Chaplin, or my father's favourites, Laurel and Hardy**, followed by some party games, some music, some dancing and food ... sandwiches, cakes and jelly. Sadly, I didn't find the parties comfortable as I knew no one, and by the time I had befriended someone, it was time to go home.

In later years we were taken to the pantomime at the Grand Theatre, but whatever the arrangements, the best part always came at the end when we were given our presents – boats for the bath, a clockwork car, some object that someone's father had expertly made (they were thrifty times), a compendium of games, dolls, or teddy bears for the toddlers, and ... balloons.

The presents were not always age-appropriate, however, and this particular year I was given a plastic army field cannon, substantial in bulk, which fired wooden shells that were the size and shape of a movie-cowboy's pistol bullets. Within a day or so my parents had decided this toy was unsuitable. Had I been spraying the living room and my mother's piano with ammunition? I don't remember, and that's memory for you – it can be selective – **but what happened next is as clear as any childhood recollection that I have...**

One bright, crisp Saturday morning, my father and I set off to return the unfortunate gun to its suppliers. We took the big red number 96 bus which glided down from the heights of Clase, zigzagging its way through Treboeth, Brynhyfryd, past the terraced houses of Manselton, and Cwmbwrla, and the gaping field that was Dyfatty, and on towards the railway station in Swansea where we stepped off and began walking along the High Street. ... past Snell's the music shop, past Lewis Lewis, past an array of men's outfitters, until we reached my favourite shop, a big, busy Woolworth's store.

The original **Woolworth's slogan had been 'everything for a sixpence'** and in the mid-fifties things were still quite cheap. No one ever argued with my father and the assistant was ready to exchange the lethal weapon for whatever I desired. I had no hesitation. I loved toy soldiers and I was amazed at how many I could get for the cannon. This was going to be one of the best days ever!

We emerged into bright sunshine and continued walking through 'town'. I can remember the market, still open-air after the war, but not much else, until we arrived at another station of sorts which served the Mumbles Train. The **'trains' were really big red and white trams** which rumbled along the railway line all around the sweep of Swansea Bay to the village of Mumbles. The double-decker carriages could carry over a hundred passengers and regularly, two were linked together at busy times.

The much-loved Mumbles train

Photo courtesy of West Glamorgan Archives

My father knew the Mumbles train well from war-time when the family were living in a road just above Underhill Park in the village, but this is the only time I can recall travelling on the line as we now lived a long way from the sea front, and anyway, buses were running on the Swansea to Mumbles Road and out-performing their clumsier if more romantic, dearly remembered rivals. **The last Mumbles train left the station in January 1960.**

We sat upstairs and I don't think I moved during the entire journey. We passed through several stopping off points as I think we were almost the only people on board. The tide was in and we seemed to be very close to the sea at times, but the sweep of the glittering bay with just a few yachts decorating the horizon transfixed my gaze. I hugged my bag of precious new soldiers to my chest.

In Mumbles we bought ice-creams – my father always preferred a 'wafer', a slab of ice-cream presented magically between two biscuits with a metal contraption – walked along the sea front and sat on a bench where we had a complete view of Swansea Bay. I loved the fact that I could see the trains moving slowly around the coast, tiny, like dinky toys, and growing gradually larger as they reached Oystermouth Station.

As we sat there, my father began to reminisce, recalling happier times and the Swansea of his youth before the War. I was too young to understand it all but some words made an everlasting impact on me. *'I loved my old town,'* he said.

I think this was the first time that I was aware of my father having had a life which predated my own. When you are very young you think your existence fulfils every moment and desire of your parents' lives. **The Second World War had a huge impact on all the Imperials**. All their hopes for their careers and their families were placed in cold storage for six years.

Yet with courage and resourcefulness they revived their choir and their lives. As recorders of the Imperials' history we have found their determination, commitment and will to entertain so inspiring and worthy of admiration and a lesson for our times...

... and Swansea too recovered its heart and spirit and we as young boys grew up in the bright, prosperous, bustling town which it became again in the 1960s. John, Phil and myself have all lived in and visited many, many places but, like our forefathers, our hearts will always lie here in our beloved town **... our city by the sea.**